The Path to Your Ascension

Rediscovering Life's Ultimate Purpose

The Path to Your Ascension

Rediscovering Life's Ultimate Purpose

Annice Booth

BASED ON THE TEACHINGS OF
MARK L. PROPHET AND ELIZABETH CLARE PROPHET

SUMMIT UNIVERSITY PRESS®

Library of Congress Card Catalog Number: 98-88846
ISBN: 0-922729-47-6

To Mark and Elizabeth Prophet,

my gurus, my teachers, my role models,

my examples and my dearest friends—

with all my love and gratitude

for showing me the path to the ascension

and telling me that I can make it if I TRY!

The future is what you make it, even as the present is what you made it. If you do not like it, God has provided a way for you to change it, and the way is through the acceptance of the currents of the ascension flame.

—*Serapis Bey*

Contents

Preface

As I sit here in my home in Montana and gaze upon the mountains covered with snow, my meditations center on the soul's ascent to God.

I am reminded of the song of the Psalmist, "I will lift up mine eyes unto the hills from whence cometh my help. My help cometh from the LORD which made heaven and earth." [1] And all I can do is cry out from a heart full of love and gratitude, "O God, you are so magnificent!"

I shall always remember the day I met Mark and Elizabeth Prophet, truly a milestone in my life. I came from a Christian Fundamentalist background and later studied the teachings of Unity. But not until I discovered the teachings of the ascended masters given through their messengers did I realize that after hundreds, perhaps thousands of lifetimes on this earth, at long last I was offered the chance to return home to God in the ascension at the close of either this or the next embodiment.

We all know that Jesus made his ascension. But what many of us have not known is that each one of us is meant to follow his example and ascend back to the heart of God, victors over time and space.

Of course, I speak here of the ascension of the soul perfected in love and not the ascent of the physical body. As the apostle Paul said, "Flesh and blood cannot inherit the kingdom of God." [2]

The Christian church has kept this great truth of the soul's ascent from us simply because many of the teachings of Jesus have been lost or mistranslated. But now, beginning in the twentieth century, the ascended masters are showing us how to walk the path to the ascension and how to overcome the trials of everyday life and transcend the limitations of our physical bodies.

We have all sensed that there must be something better than

the life we are leading but we haven't quite known how to find that something better. I have learned much truth over the years through my study of the masters' words and by pondering the mysteries of life in my heart. This book is an attempt to explain what I have learned in simple terms.

From my very first contact with the ascended masters, I knew their teachings were true. Mark Prophet once told me to trust my intuition and listen to my heart. So what I am offering you in this book is what my heart has confirmed and what I have endeavored to apply in my own life.

This book on the path to the ascension is drawn from lectures that I gave at Summit University over the past twenty years. It has also been inspired by memories of my experiences with the masters in their etheric retreats.

I have made no attempt to write in an erudite literary style. Instead I have been deliberately conversational, just as though you had invited me into your living room and we were sitting before the fire discussing the path to the ascension.

In this book we will follow a group of souls who meet nightly at the Ascension Retreat while their bodies are asleep. Serapis Bey, the master who presides over the Ascension Temple, employs an interactive method of teaching his students who aspire to be candidates for the ascension. I invite you to join us.

At the back of the book, you will find a glossary of esoteric terms, and I have also included there a bibliography of books and tapes for further study.

You may choose to complete the exercises included in the workbook. They provide an opportunity to assess your progress on the path to the ascension and they guide you to see some aspects of your personality that may need attention.

As often happens in private conversations with fellow seekers, I have emphasized the keys that I feel are significant. You might find it helpful to underline certain passages in the text and make a list of those points that you feel are keys to your own ascension.

I am writing this book out of my gratitude to the masters for having been fortunate enough to discover these great truths. I also write it because God's love impels me to share with you what I know can give you your ultimate freedom and immortality. It is my hope that through these pages God will speak to your heart as the ascended masters have spoken to mine.

May God richly bless you,

Annice Booth

CHAPTER ONE

❧

Finding the Purpose of Life

*T*his is the story of the soul—your soul, my soul, millions of souls who are searching for immortality. We all know that there is something more to life than the physical, everyday existence we are leading. But what is that something? How do we achieve it? Where do we begin?

Come with me as we search for answers in the teachings of the great masters of wisdom. First, let us understand that the journey did not just begin in this lifetime. We are old souls, and this is the first lesson the masters teach us.

We have lived in many ages and in many climes. We have been saints and sinners. We have been young and old. We have had lives of wealth and lives of poverty; we have had lives of success and lives of failure, lives of beauty and lives of degradation. We have seen civilizations rise and fall.

In fact, to be as near the end of our search as I believe we are today, we have looked far and wide and have learned many lessons. We have also failed some lessons and have had to take them over again.

In this lifetime we stand at the threshold of immortality, ready to be taught the truth that we must transcend physical existence and make our ascension into the Light from which we came.

The Etheric Realm

We descended to earth a spirit spark from God and now, at long last, we are being offered a glimpse into the heaven-world of our origin. This higher world, although not visible to our outer sight, is peopled with myriad beings glowing with light and love—mighty archangels, angels, Elohim, cosmic beings and ascended masters, tiny elementals (nature spirits) and great beings of the elements who are masters of earth, air, fire and water.

The realm of the ascended masters can only be seen through the eyes of the soul as we raise our consciousness and center in our hearts. These great masters have offered to teach us a path that contains the necessary steps to find our way back to God's heart.

They teach our souls, either while our bodies sleep at night or during the time between embodiments. During the day, we are busily occupied with the necessary activities of daily life—working at our job, caring for our home and children, studying at school or university. Only in rare moments of quiet and meditation can our souls reach up to the etheric realm where the masters reside.

An Invitation

Our souls have been offered the great gift of being taught personally in the retreats by the great masters of wisdom. These retreats, called the Universities of the Spirit, are located on the etheric plane, a level above the physical that vibrates at such a high frequency that our eyes cannot see it. Yet the etheric realm is as concrete and real to the eyes of the soul as the physical world is to our normal eyesight.

The ascended masters who are our teachers have been men and women just as you and I are today. They have walked the earth throughout the ages and then, having mastered their energies and their environment, have ascended back to God. They faced the same problems we face today and have overcome them. Yes, Jesus was only one of many who demonstrated the ascension.

The masters have offered us the advantage of their attainment to help shorten our journey to immortality. All who sincerely desire to follow the path to the ascension are invited to attend these Universities of the Spirit, especially those who are willing to follow the precepts the masters teach. So come with me tonight. Let's go to bed early this night so that our souls can travel in their finer bodies to the Ascension Temple over Luxor, Egypt.

Although the remains of a physical temple still exist at Luxor, we will be attending the spiritual retreat that is superimposed over the physical ruins. The flame of the Ascension is focused here, as Serapis Bey carried it to this location before the sinking of Atlantis.

Our souls are invited to come in their light-bodies to experience the first lesson that the Ascended Master Serapis Bey, the master of the Ascension Temple, will teach. He will be our teacher tonight and for some time to come.

The First Class

We find ourselves in a beautiful white room with sparkling gold flakes in the walls. We feel the pulsations of the steely white fire of the ascension flame in another room that we are not yet qualified to enter. We realize that there are many other rooms in this complex that are used for specific initiations leading to the ascension. Other classrooms like ours are set aside for more advanced instruction.

A door opens and our teacher enters. Serapis Bey is clothed in a white linen robe that sparkles with light so dazzlingly bright that even the eyes of our soul can scarcely look upon him. A large yellow topaz secures his turban.

Serapis surveys the room with a warm smile of welcome and begins to speak.

"Greetings, devotees of my heart!

"It is important for you to come for assistance to our etheric retreat at Luxor as you strive to win your ascension both at inner and outer levels. In this way, you can apply what you have learned out of the body to your daily tasks and to your family relationships.

"From time to time I shall assign tutors to work with you and help you correct every step you may have missed on the

Path. Many other ascended masters have agreed to help me school your souls. You will enjoy meeting them, I am sure.

"And now, let us begin with the question you all have on your hearts at this time."

As we sit at his feet, the question we have been asking ourselves is What is the purpose of life? Serapis knows the answer, *"It is to prepare yourself for the ascension.*

"The future is what you make it, even as the present is what you made it. If you do not like it, God has provided a way for you to change it, and the way is through the acceptance of the currents of the ascension flame."[1]

This simple truth spoken by the Ascended Master Serapis Bey is perhaps the most important concept we will ever hear at the Ascension Temple in Luxor. More questions come to our mind but at the moment this answer is sufficient for our meditation.

Reincarnation

Let's consider what the master meant when he said, "the present is what you made it."

Serapis is teaching us the doctrine of reincarnation, a truth that is fundamental to our understanding of the path to the ascension. Reincarnation teaches that what we did in our previous lives has affected our present life today. It explains the seeming inequities of life, why some souls are born crippled or blind, why some have great creativity and special talents from an early age, why some struggle throughout their life just to eke out a living and why burdensome events occur in some lives whereas happy and carefree events fill the lives of others.

We realize as we ponder his statement, "The future is what you make it," that this implies many of us must change our habits and our lifestyle. For to have the future we would like, we need a physical body as purified as possible. We need a healthy diet, exercise, sufficient rest, quiet time for meditation and prayer each day and a sincere desire to change our life.

His next sentence, "If you do not like it, God has provided a way for you to change it, and the way is through the acceptance of the currents of the ascension flame," shows us that we really need to find out what the ascension is.

But our master says that this first lesson is enough for tonight. He wants us to meditate upon what he has given us and apply it in our daily life before we return to class again.

When we awaken the next day, most of us cannot remember the time we spent in the master's retreat or the lesson we learned. However, our soul knows and remembers, for it is the soul the master is teaching.

As we go about our daily life, performing the same mundane tasks as always, something seems different. We feel more peaceful as though relieved of some of our previous stress.

Turning these new ideas over in our minds, we find that to fully assimilate the master's teachings we need to set aside any preconceived notions, any doctrines or dogmas, worries, cares, concerns or questions we might have. We need to let our soul speak to us so that we may enter the happy state we once knew before we became entangled in the web of life on earth. Our soul has known from the beginning that her ultimate purpose is to ascend back home to God.

If we sincerely embark on this search for immortality, it can easily become an all-consuming task. But there is one pitfall we need to avoid, for El Morya, another of our ascended master teachers, says, "Your spirituality is expressed by your practicality."

The plan is not for us to become hermits or recluses, concerned only with our ascension and concentrating on our spiritual life to the exclusion of our other responsibilities. The masters teach the middle way of avoidance of both fanaticism and indulgence as did Gautama Buddha.

To fully absorb the masters' teachings, we must be well-rounded students, fully integrated in the world today and yet somewhat apart from it. As Jesus taught his disciples to be in the world but not of it, that is our assignment also.

When Serapis Bey first came into the room, he appeared as a flame of white fire representing the great spirit of the discipline of the law. At the conclusion of the lesson, after he had established his presence with us, we saw him leave as a whirling, pink flame.

The delicate shade of this pink flame of love coming after the white fire of the ascension flame that he bears, shows the gentleness and the intensity of the love of Serapis Bey.

∿ *If you wish to further enhance your study before proceeding to Chapter 2, you will find exercises on p. 218.*

🕊

CHAPTER TWO

What Is the Ascension?

At last the long-awaited moment when our souls can attend our second class at the Ascension Temple has come! The master warned us to be patient and told us that we could not assimilate all the steps to immortality at once. But we are excited, for we now know that liberation is in sight.

Serapis Bey is our instructor for these introductory steps to the ascension. And well he should be, for he is the Master of the Ascension Temple at Luxor, Egypt.

As the master steps up to the lectern, he says with a smile, "Tonight I am sure you wish me to answer the question you asked the last time we met, 'What is the ascension?'

"I cannot give you a simple answer, but I will present a few ideas for you to meditate on. I shall intersperse them from time to time with other instruction. Pay close attention so that you do not miss any of the keys to your ascension."

Keys to the Ascension

Serapis explains to us that the ascension in the light is our victorious return home to God. From the beginning it has been the goal of all life on earth.

The ascension is an upward spiraling that affects the entire being of man; yet the ascension currents can hurt no one. Through the flame of the ascension, we become one with our Higher Self and then with God the Father, our own I AM Presence. We are then filled with the light of the spiritual sun and can no longer remain bound to the gravitational pull of the earth.

As the unlimited power of God surges through our being, we will have no further need for a physical body. We will have transcended the limitations of time and space.

When we say, "God the Father," understand that we see God

as our Father-Mother God who is both masculine and feminine. Since gender-neutral language can be cumbersome and at times confusing, we shall use the pronouns *he* and *him* to refer to the Father-Mother God and in general to all individuals. In no way do we intend to exclude women or the feminine aspect of the Godhead.

And while we are about it, we shall use the pronouns *she* and *her* to refer to the soul, because each soul, whether housed in a male or female body, is the feminine complement of the masculine Spirit.

Even if you happen to be in a man's body this time around, your soul is feminine, and both men and women have masculine and feminine traits and characteristics.

The I AM Presence

Before I proceed further, I should like to explain the term *I AM Presence*. We will be using this name for God throughout our classes and I want to be sure you understand the true meaning of it. The I AM Presence is the individualized Presence of God focused for each individual soul. It is the God-identity of the individual.

I AM is the name of God given to Moses in the Old Testament. When he was asked to speak to the Israelites, Moses asked God what name he should use. God said, "I AM THAT I AM. Thus shalt thou say unto the children of Israel, I AM hath sent me unto you.... This is my name forever, and this is my memorial unto all generations."[1]

When we say "I AM" we mean "God in me is." We should be careful to complete the sentence with only positive thoughts, because we are putting the power of God's name into those thoughts.

The Dossier on the Ascension

Serapis tells us that he has written the *Dossier on the Ascension,* a book for present-day seekers. He says that he has included in it much of the instruction that he gives to souls in his etheric retreat when they are apart from their physical bodies. It also includes much of the training he is giving to us individually.

Serapis offers us these words from the Dossier.

"You need not expect, precious ones, that as the swoop of a great bird of paradise, Heaven will come down to you and raise you instantly up into the light. Each day you weave a strand of light substance back to the heart of your Presence by the shuttle of your attention. Each strand strengthens the anchor beyond the veil and thus draws you into a state of consciousness wherein God can use you more as an effective instrument for good.

"Let all understand, then, that the ascension is won just as much by good works and devotion to God, by service to your fellow men, by service to the light, by decrees offered for and on behalf of mankind, by healing service to those who require it, and by the many avenues of the Brotherhood, as it is won by a direct study of the mechanical process involved in the final ritual of the ascension itself."[2]

Then Serapis gives us another major key from the Dossier: "There is no need to have a sense of struggle but only a sense of acceptance."[3] Saint Germain, another ascended master who will teach us as our class progresses, has also said more than once, "It is the sense of struggle that makes the struggle."

Serapis would like us to meditate on this concept.

The Sense of Struggle

Much of the sense of struggle in our lives can be removed from us if we would be simple, childlike and accept our ascension as a gift of God. We could just say, "Thank you, Father. I want my ascension. I want it in divine order, according to divine direction and the will of God, whenever it will do the most good for the planet."

Often we push away the good that comes to us by saying, "I am not worthy." Yet a little child can accept a gift eagerly, with gladness and joy. We have been offered the ascension as a gift from God. And it is ours to accept with the same joy as a little child—not questioning why this gift was given to us or whether we are worthy of it.

Saint Germain has made us the promise that if we apply the law, we can ascend in this lifetime. If we require another incarnation to fulfill our divine plan or our karma, we may make our ascension in the next life.

You must believe you can ascend. You have to ask for it. You have to work for it, and you have to accept it as a reality here and now, subject to when the Lords of Karma and your Higher Self want you to make your ascension. The ascension is the fulfilling of the law of God for every man.

The Lords of Karma

The Lords of Karma are a body of eight ascended beings of great attainment who form the Karmic Board. They dispense justice to this system of worlds, adjudicating karma, mercy and judgment on behalf of all who live on this earth.

All souls appear before the Karmic Board prior to each incarnation on earth to receive their assignment and karmic allotment for that lifetime. Following each incarnation, the soul again appears before the Karmic Board for a review of her performance.

These masters determine which souls will embody, when they will be born and where on the planet they will live. The Lords of Karma assign souls to families and communities, measuring out the weight of karma that must be balanced.

The Karmic Board, together with the person's I AM Presence and Christ Self, determines when the soul has earned the right to be free from the wheel of karma and the round of rebirth.

The entire record of all our past lives and our momentums of both good and evil must be counted. And when we have brought at least 51 percent of all the energy that has ever been allotted to us into balance with the purity and harmony of our God Self, we may be offered the gift of the ascension.

As we ponder this information, the master tells us that we will discuss the subject of karma in depth in a later session.

From time to time, Serapis Bey invites other ascended masters in addition to Saint Germain to enter the retreat and teach. Such a master is Lord Lanto, who has great attainment on the wisdom ray.

Lanto speaks briefly. *"Each day is an opportunity for the soul to attain an element of her eternal mastery. You do not pass in one moment from the human octave to the divine, but step by step you climb wisdom's golden stairs."* [4]

The Ascension Is a Gift from God

In reality man is a flaming spirit who descended into physical form to master the conditions and trials of everyday life and his own lower self. When he has successfully overcome the human will, the human ego, the human intellect and has replaced them with their divine components, he can then ascend back to the heart of the Father—victor over time and space.

The ascension is the gift of God. It is given to us more by his grace than by our works, although both are necessary.

Membership in any specific church does not in itself guarantee our ascension. Devotees from all races and religions have been granted the gift of the ascension when certain requirements, (which we will discuss later), have been met.

The ascension flame is a flame of hope. We have hope because we have within us the divine memory of the ascension of Jesus the Christ. Our souls remember that Mary, the Mother of Jesus, and others who are unknown and unsung have also followed in Jesus' footsteps as the true heroes and heroines of the world.

Jesus' ascension is the matrix of the ascension of every other soul. His life was meant to be an example to us, and we are intended to ascend as he did. The mysteries of God's creation are many, and Jesus unveiled for us one of life's greatest mysteries.

The ascension is God's desire for every one, and so all of Heaven stands ready to assist the man, woman or child who seeks to express his or her true identity as a son or daughter of God. All life should welcome the opportunity we have been given to follow in the Master's footsteps. Jesus was a wayshower, one of many.

One of the lessons we learn this second night is that there are many more ascended beings than there are men and women living on earth now. We find that the Bible records but a few of the many who have ascended into the light.

The Ascended Beings

Men have ascended from all walks of life and from all the world's major religions. Enoch, the seventh from Adam, "walked with God: and he was not; for God took him."[5] Elijah ascended into heaven in a "chariot of fire."[6] Gautama Buddha achieved Paranirvana at the end of a long life of teaching his disciples. Mary, the Mother of Jesus, was assumed into heaven in the first century A.D. Padmasambhava, the ninth-century Tibetan teacher, took flight to his paradise at the conclusion of his life. We also know that Melchizedek, John the Beloved and Saint Thérèse of Lisieux ascended. But these are only a few of the many ascended saints and hosts of heaven. The sons and daughters of God throughout cosmos have been following the path of the ascension since the creation because it is the path of spiritual evolution.

The difference in vibratory rate between the human world and the ascended masters' realm makes it impossible for many to see the great hosts of heaven; but there are untold numbers of ascended beings who want to help the earth and await our prayers.

The problem is that our eyesight, vibrating at the level of earth, cannot see into the etheric realms and the heaven world because our normal range of vision vibrates only from the infrared to the ultraviolet spectrums. But there are some in embodiment who have clairvoyant vision and therefore can see the beauty of the inner realms.

The Law of Octaves

By the law of octaves, the ascended masters, angels and cosmic beings cannot enter our lives until they are invoked by us. We asked God for free will. He gave us that free will and we departed from our perfection, determined to lead our own lives. It has taken us many, many centuries to realize that perhaps we have made a mess of it. Now it is time to straighten things out and return to the Father.

Often we make more karma in a particular lifetime than we are able to balance. For it is possible to lose some of our good karma by outbursts of anger and other negative emotions. This certainly is a valid reason to keep a daily check on our thoughts, emotions and actions.

The kingdom of heaven is without end, and those who enter into the ascension are soon assigned to other tasks in the service of the light. Never fear that the ascension flame will cancel out your identity. Instead, it offers you a glorious new life. The main difference between life on earth and life in heaven is that in heaven the individual has infinite time and infinite energy at his command.

The entire class applauds as we realize the possibilities that are open to us. Each one thinks to himself, "Just imagine what a blessing it would be to have all the time I need to perform my spiritual tasks and never be tired again!"

We all straighten up in our seats and listen eagerly, certain now that we have found the Path for which we have been searching for centuries.

The Last Enemy to Be Overcome Is Death

Serapis Bey speaks to an eager class listening closely to his every word. He says that the last enemy to be overcome is death. Death is the absolute opposite of the ascension spiral. It is life that is reality not death.

Jesus proved conclusively that there is no death. Using the

resurrection flame and then later the ascension currents, he proved life to be the natural and death the unnatural state of being.

Remember that Jesus said, "Let not your heart be troubled: you believe in God, believe also in me. In my Father's house are many mansions; if it were not so, I would have told you. I go to prepare a place for you. And if I go and prepare a place for you, I will come again and receive you unto myself; that where I am, there ye may be also." [7]

Jesus expected us to follow in his footsteps when he said, "He that believeth on me, the works that I do shall he do also; and greater works than these shall he do because I go unto my Father." [8] Our assignment, direct from the Master, is to conquer the limitations of our physical bodies and ascend back to the Father as he did, victors over time and space.

Jesus wanted us to follow his example—to do as he had done and not to believe that he was the only one who could ascend to God.

We realize, then, at the conclusion of the night's lecture that when we come to the retreat at Luxor as a candidate for the ascension, we are coming for the grand finale of our sojourn of hundreds and thousands of years on this earth.

Our souls rejoice that we are worthy to receive this promise of immortality and we all vow silently to make this our final incarnation on earth if it be the will of God for us.

~ *If you wish to further enhance your study before proceeding to Chapter 3, you will find exercises on p. 219.*

CHAPTER THREE

❦

The Masters, East and West

We gather a bit early this evening, looking for an opportunity to discuss among ourselves the masters' teachings. We all seem to have a question that is not quite clear to us and we are determined to ask the master at our first opportunity.

An immediate sense of expectation fills the room as Serapis Bey enters and takes his place at the lectern. With a smile he says, "I think perhaps a bit of review might be in order before we proceed with our subject tonight. I sense some questions on your minds. Who would like to be first?"

This is just the opportunity we had hoped for. One young woman rises and says, "Beloved Serapis, you have mentioned the term ascended master *several times and yet some of us still don't have a clear picture of what an ascended master is. Could you please explain further and maybe even tell us a little bit about several of the masters whom you have mentioned?"*

The master says, "That is an excellent question and I am glad that you asked it. Feel free as we progress to ask any questions that arise in your mind, any point of the teaching about which you are not quite clear."

Ascended Masters

Serapis tells us that to be an ascended master is the opportunity the soul was given when she was created. The ascended masters are simply people who have walked the earth as we are now doing and who have reentered the consciousness of God. They are the saints "clothed in white robes"[1] mentioned in Revelation. They have faced the same problems and trials, grief and joy as we are facing today.

Ascended masters are important to us because they have

proven cosmic laws that we are in the process of proving. They know we can make it, because they made it—often in more difficult situations than the ones we face today. In the dark ages of the world's history, the ascended masters were forbidden to serve as teachers of mortals. Each one on earth who ascended in those times had to walk by faith and he succeeded only by expanding the love flame that burned within his heart.

A master is one who has mastered the energies of the self—the energies that flow and course through the being of man and woman. A master is one who has mastered his environment, his world. And that mastery—reaching a certain level and bringing the soul into congruency with his own Higher Self and his own God-awareness—propelled that one into the reunion with God that is called the ascension in the light.

The ascended masters have gained the victory over sin, disease, death and over every conflict. They have balanced what in the East is called karma and in the West, sin. They have balanced all the energy that was ever given to them in all incarnations and have returned to the heart of the I AM Presence and now are a part of the ascended saints in heaven.

As the living spirits of God who minister to the children of God on earth, the masters point the way and they say, "I AM the way. This is the way and the way ye know."

They show us that the way can be followed and that by proving the laws of God we too can attain immortality. All that we strive for and all that we are is not lost at the moment of death, for the ascension is the proof that death, the last enemy, can be overcome.

We are thrilled to hear that each of us can become an ascended master! With a smile Serapis says, "Before we learn about specific masters, I would like you to have an explanation of a term we often use: The Great White Brotherhood."

The Great White Brotherhood

The Great White Brotherhood is an order of ascended beings serving in this system of worlds. It is a union of ascended masters who have graduated not only from this planet but also from other planets in this solar system and other systems in the galaxy.

Who, then, are the members of the Great White Brotherhood? They are the saints and sages of all ages. They are from East and West. They are the great spiritual lights, the artists and the unsung heroes—people from every walk of life. They do not have a particular religion or a particular creed except love and obedience and sacrifice. They have come through all paths that lead back to the Source and the One.

The word *white* refers not to race but to the white light of the Christ, the aura, that surrounds these saints and sages "robed in white," who have risen from every nation and every age to be counted among the immortals.

"Now I should like to acquaint you with two ascended masters," says Serapis, "Saint Germain and El Morya.

"These two ascended masters are well qualified to teach the path of overcoming. Their lives on earth were even more challenging than yours are today (even though you believe the present time to be full of trials). You will soon see that many of the lives of these masters are well known to you through-out both secular history and the history of the Church."

Serapis warns us that he may be using some terms which are unfamiliar to us. He suggests that we make a note of them. During the question and answer period he will gladly explain. He also suggests that we even might wish to keep a notebook of any spiritual or esoteric terms that are new to us. In this way, by the end of the course, we will have a glossary of ascended master terms. *

He begins by telling us that our souls have known El Morya throughout the ages even though his name seems new to us at present. Many of us have been with him in several of his embodiments throughout history, for souls have a tendency to reembody in groups.

Some of the students had wondered why everyone in this class seemed familiar! And here is the answer. Our group is

---

*See the glossary in the back of the book pp. 245–252.

*together once again at the Ascension Temple, sitting at the feet
of the Ascended Master Serapis Bey, learning about El Morya!*

El Morya

The Ascended Master El Morya holds the office of the Lord of
the First Ray of the Will of God. His retreat, the Temple of Good
Will, is located in the etheric realm in the foothills of the
Himalayas above the city of Darjeeling, India. He presides there
as Chief of the Darjeeling Council of the Great White
Brotherhood. His keynote is contained in the melody of Edward
Elgar's first *Pomp and Circumstance* march—the one we know
as "The Land of Hope and Glory."

The Brothers of the Diamond Heart who serve at this retreat
assist human endeavors by organizing, developing and imple-
menting the will of God as the foundation for all successful
movements. El Morya's diamond-shining mind of God is the
very heart of any endeavor.

Faith, power, joy, constancy, strength, protection, perfection,
love of the will of God and a desire to do the will of our Father
are qualities of the first ray.

El Morya conducts classes at his Temple of Good Will for
statesmen, leaders and organizers, those who are cooperating
with the masters in their efforts to assist in the stabilization of the
governments and economies of the nations.

In 1958 El Morya founded The Summit Lighthouse as a
means of spreading the teachings of the ascended masters to the
lightbearers of the world. He trained and sponsored Mark and
Elizabeth Prophet as messengers through whom the masters
could dictate their teachings.

El Morya's devotion to the will of God can be seen throughout his many lives of service to mankind both in government and
in the Church. One of his early embodiments was that of Melchior,
one of the three wise men who attended the birth of Jesus. In the
sixth century he was embodied as Arthur, King of the Britons,
who founded the order of the Knights of the Round Table.

In the twelfth century El Morya was Thomas à Becket, who served as Lord Chancellor of England and then Archbishop of Canterbury under Henry II. In the late fifteenth century he was embodied as Sir Thomas More who wrote *Utopia*. In this lifetime he again was Lord Chancellor of England under Henry VIII. Both as Thomas à Becket and as Sir Thomas More he was martyred because he refused to compromise his integrity to please the king.

As Akbar the Great in the sixteenth century, El Morya founded the Mogul Empire in India and was the greatest of its rulers. In the nineteenth century he was known and loved as the Irish poet, Thomas Moore, among whose ballads the best remembered is "Believe Me, If All Those Endearing Young Charms."

His final embodiment in India in the latter part of the nineteenth century was as the Rajput prince El Morya Khan. In 1875, working closely with Kuthumi and Djwal Kul (the other wise men), Serapis Bey and other masters, he attempted to acquaint the West with the reality of the invisible world by sponsoring The Theosophical Society.

Since his ascension in about 1898, El Morya has worked tirelessly with Saint Germain for the cause of world and individual freedom.

Saint Germain

Just as Jesus was the Master of the Piscean dispensation for the last two thousand years, so now Saint Germain is earth's Master of Freedom for the next two-thousand-year period known as the Aquarian age. Jesus and Saint Germain work closely together to bring true freedom to all. There is no competition between them, nor does our acknowledgment of Saint Germain as the Aquarian master in any way ignore Jesus' great sacrifice and service to the world.

It is important that we give Jesus his proper love and respect as our Saviour. He is now an ascended master and is working closely with others of the Brotherhood to continue to bring the true teachings to us again in the twentieth century and in a form that people of today can understand and accept.

He is still our Jesus whom we loved and worshipped two thousand years ago and he is as close to us today as he was in Galilee. We can pour our love and gratitude to Jesus for his Galilean ministry and still accept Saint Germain as the Lord of the Seventh Ray of freedom, ritual, mercy and transmutation today.

In fact, Jesus himself foretold the coming of Saint Germain in this age in the tenth chapter of Revelation. There Saint Germain is referred to as the "seventh angel" who will finish the mysteries of God. Saint Germain has chosen to reveal himself to us by a name that simply means "holy brother" from the Latin *sanctus germanus.*

Over seventy thousand years ago, Saint Germain was the emperor-king of a great golden-age civilization that existed where the Sahara Desert is now. Under his enlightened reign, the entire civilization knew an era of peace, abundance and accomplishments in education and the arts and sciences.

However, a portion of the people gradually became more interested in the gratification of the outer senses than in fulfilling the divine plan for that golden age. This eventually caused them to lose their powers of God-mastery and Saint Germain was asked by the Karmic Board to withdraw as their leader.

His life as Samuel the Prophet of the tribe of Levi and priest of the temple (eleventh century B.C.), is recorded in the First Book of Samuel. Centuries later when he overshadowed the early American patriots and helped to draft the Constitution and shape the destiny of America, he became known as "Uncle Sam."

As Joseph, the father of Jesus, he was chosen to be the protector of Jesus and Mary. Saint Joseph is still considered to be the patron of fathers and of families. In the first century Saint Germain was Saint Alban, the first of the Christian martyrs of Britain. In the fifth century he was known as Proclus, a Greek philosopher, teacher of metaphysics and the highly honored successor of Plato as head of the Academy at Athens.

The story of his embodiment as Merlin the Magician is recorded in the folk tales of nearly every European nation. According to Malory's account in *Le Morte d'Arthur,* Merlin stands highly revered as the king's counselor, at times disguised in order to convey an imminent message, warning or initiation.

As Roger Bacon in the thirteenth century, Saint Germain was a prominent English philosopher and experimental scientist. Later he became a Franciscan monk. He produced a vast encyclopedia of all the known sciences, including his unique understanding of alchemy and experimental studies, many of these works being written in a secret cipher.

His lifetime as Christopher Columbus is familiar to all. But we are not as familiar with the life of Francis Bacon, another of Saint Germain's major embodiments. Bacon was Lord Chancellor of England, statesman, essayist, the "father of inductive science."

His numerous philosophical works, including *Novus Organum* and *New Atlantis,* form integral parts of a grand comprehensive scheme for the restoration of wisdom and a golden-age culture. Recent research has revealed Francis Bacon as the true author of the Shakespearean plays. He also organized the translation of the King James Version of the Bible.

Francis Bacon sponsored the early society of the Rosy Cross, the Rosicrucian Order, and was instrumental in the founding of the Masonic Order. This beloved master has had many more embodiments of service dedicated to the flame of freedom.

Saint Germain won his ascension on May 1, 1684, after having made, as he once commented, "two million right decisions" during thousands of years of service on behalf of earth and her evolutions.

After his ascension, by a special dispensation, he appeared in Europe in the eighteenth and nineteenth centuries as Le Comte de Saint Germain, the "Wonderman of Europe." He worked behind the scenes to bring about a United States of Europe and forestall the horrors of the French Revolution. When his work was proven unsuccessful, he turned his attention to the new nation of America and became the sponsor of the United States at inner levels.

With a twinkle in his eye, Serapis asks, "Now, do you feel you know these masters a little better? Have you been with them in some of their lives? I suspect that is the case."

At this moment a tall master strides into the room and asks politely if he may briefly address the students. Serapis acquiesces and moves aside.

This shining being of Light turns to us with a smile and says, "Now, dear hearts, there is one more ascended master about whom you need to know tonight, and I am sure he is so humble that he will not talk about himself. I speak of the Ascended Master Serapis Bey.

"Serapis is a being of great love. He is a disciplinarian, there is no question about that, for he embodies the white ray of discipline and detail. However, his capacity for love is so great that instead of going on to cosmic service, Serapis has remained with earth's evolutions, teaching about the ascension. Without him, many of us would just slide by and say, 'Thanks, but I'll just wait for another embodiment.' We call Serapis' technique the 'push-pull' technique, for he is reaching down to pull you up, and you are pushing up to reach him.

"It is unfortunate that the average person does not know about the ascension or that he has the opportunity to ascend. He knows Jesus ascended, but has probably no idea that he is supposed to follow Jesus' example and achieve his own ascension in the light."

The tall master asks if we would like to hear about a few of Serapis Bey's embodiments before he became Master of the Ascension Temple. We all applaud enthusiastically and settle down in anticipation of this information.

Serapis Bey

The service to life that Serapis has chosen is to prepare disciples for the ritual of the ascension. Individuals are admitted to his retreat only after they have successfully passed certain initiations. These are given by other members of the ascended hierarchy who act as the sponsors and teachers of unascended initiates.

As you know, Serapis Bey is an ascended master who resides here in the Ascension Temple in the etheric octave over Luxor, Egypt. He tutors your souls while your bodies are asleep at night and between embodiments. He is the Lord of the Fourth Ray of Purity and the Ascension.

On Atlantis, Serapis Bey was a priest in the Ascension Temple. He carried the ascension flame up the Nile River to Luxor just before Atlantis sank. For the most part, his major embodiments have been in Egypt, guarding and nourishing the ascension flame for all mankind.

In the fourteenth century B.C. Serapis was Amenhotep III who built the temple at Karnak. And in the sixth century B.C. he was embodied as Phidias, the Athenian architect and sculptor who designed the Parthenon and supervised its construction. As Leonidas, King of Sparta, he paid with his life at the Pass of Thermopylae in 480 B.C., rather than yield to the Persians.

In about 400 B.C. Serapis Bey accepted his own immortal victory, the ascension in the light. Serapis has legions of seraphim at his command. They are the beautiful, tall angels who serve at the Ascension Temple.

The tall master now turns to Serapis and says, "May I proceed and explain to these students your methods of discipline?" Serapis bows, "If you wish, please continue."

We listen a bit apprehensively, as we are a little uneasy about how much discipline we can endure.

Methods of Discipline

The tall master explains to us that Serapis Bey's methods of discipline "are tailor-made for each candidate for the ascension.

After an initial interview by himself or one of the Twelve Adepts presiding in his mystery school, devotees who come to his retreat are assigned in groups of five or more to carry out projects with other initiates whose karmic patterns ... forecast the *maximum* friction between their lifestreams. Each group must serve together until they become harmonious—individually and as a coherent unit of hierarchy—learning all the while that those character traits that are most offensive in others are the polar opposite of their own worst faults and that what one criticizes in another is apt to be the root of his own misery.

"Aside from this type of group dynamics, individuals are placed in situations (both in the retreat and in their day-to-day activities) that provide them with the greatest challenges, according to their changing karmic patterns. In this course, a student cannot simply up and leave a crisis, a circumstance or an individual who is not to his liking. He must stand, face and conquer his own carnal mind and misqualified energy by disciplining his consciousness in the art of nonreaction to the human creation of others, even as he learns how not to be dominated or influenced by his own human creation."[2]

Serapis teaches artists, musicians, sculptors, architects, planners—those who serve on the fourth ray as well as the most staunch disciples of every ray—to express purity, harmony, rhythm, balance and perfection in any undertaking. He clarifies the rigors of the highest path to attainment, the path of the white light, through service, self-sacrifice and surrender to God.

He has great attainment in divine geometry and design and assists his disciples in the self-disciplines that are necessary to the ascension. He trains them to portray their Higher Self, or Christ Self, for service and attainment in the world of form. He also shows the aspirant how to discipline past momentums of negative spirals that would stand in the way of the ascension flame.

The ascension flame is an intense fiery white with a crystal glow. The Easter lily is the symbol of the flame and its focus in the nature kingdom. The white diamond is its focus in the mineral kingdom. The melody of the flame is the "Triumphal March" from Giuseppe Verdi's *Aïda*, and the keynote of the retreat is "Liebesträume" by Franz Liszt. The melody of "Celeste Aïda" contains Serapis Bey's own keynote.

The master who has been our guest this night graciously bows to each one and says, "Thank you for your attention. Now I will return the lectern to Serapis Bey. I think he would like to tell you more about the Ascension Temple and Retreat himself. May God richly bless you all."

Serapis thanks him for his assistance tonight but declines to include instruction on the Ascension Retreat during this session, preferring to wait until we have received more instruction on the initiations of the ascension.

"However," the master says, "before we conclude our class this evening, I would like you to learn about some of the other masters who serve ascension's flame."

The Masters of the Ascension

Greatest of all the beings who serve on the fourth ray of Purity and the Ascension are the Elohim Purity and Astrea. Next are the archangels Gabriel and Hope; Hope is Gabriel's archeia, or twin flame. All the fourth-ray angels as well as the legions of purity—including the Goddess of Purity, the Goddess of Light and the Queen of Light—stand ready and willing to teach you and help you make your ascension. But, by cosmic law, they cannot enter your world until they are invited.

(The term Goddess is a name that these great beings have earned because of their wholehearted and complete identification with the light and the flame of purity. Please understand that these are not the old pagan gods and goddesses. These lady masters are ascended beings of great stature and attainment.)

Of special importance in their dedication to the ascension flame are the seraphim, and their captain is the magnificent being Justinius. The Seraphim are an order of angels dedicated to focusing the flame, or consciousness, of purity in the Great

Central Sun and throughout cosmos. They serve the ascension flame and the Ascension Temple and have a twenty-four-hour-a-day commitment to service.

These angelic beings are mighty in height, for they are accustomed to the dimensions of other worlds. They are flaming spirits of living fire who possess the ability to interpenetrate matter. Millions of seraphim make their cyclic rounds throughout this galaxy once every twenty-four hours.

We may call to the seraphim to tarry with us as they sweep around the earth. They are able to interpenetrate our forms and leave within our auras their residue of cosmic purity. This residue resembles the sacred ash precipitated in the hands of a holy man and is actually a white-fire ash from the Great Central Sun.

Serapis has commented on the seraphim in his *Dossier on the Ascension.* "I know of no power more valiantly capable of assisting anyone into his own ascension than the transmutative efforts toward Cosmic Christ purity which are emitted by the seraphic hosts.

"In our retreat at Luxor, the meditations upon the seraphim are a very important part of our spiritual instruction. Jesus himself spent a great deal of time in communion with the seraphic hosts. This allowed him to develop the superior power whereby he could cast out demons and take dominion over the outer world of form."

Justinius, Captain of Seraphic Hosts

At this point, Justinius, the leader of the seraphim, enters our lecture hall, flashing light and love. Serapis welcomes him and says, "Won't you please take over and explain the service of your seraphim?" Justinius agrees and we all sit a little straighter as Justinius begins to speak.

"If you could penetrate the illustrations of Gustav Doré of angelic scenes across the cosmos, you would see that even the suggestion from the pen of the artist of an infinite multitude of heavenly hosts cannot begin to show how cosmos is

packed with the beings of light, of cherubim and seraphim.

"*We, the seraphim, come to make you pure and clean, to make you whole. We come to minister to the soul. And so we come, passing through the microcosm, and our fire burns the cause of disease, of poison, of the toxins that have been passing through you for so many years in the food, the water, the tobacco and the alcohol that mankind imbibe.*

"*Who, pray tell, will keep your souls alive and evolving in these body temples if not the angels who come to minister, who come to uplift? I tell you, mankind has been spared again and again and again the last plague and all forms of chaos and disturbance and imbalance and insanity by the very presence of angels.*

"*Now hear this! When we pass through your forms as spirits of living fire, we leave, as it were, the calling card of our identity, a focus of fire tingeing your aura with a hue of the Central Sun, tingeing the aura with a halo. And for a while, then, there is that glow, that essence, that sense of well-being, that inner warmth.*"

Justinius then suggests that we concentrate on learning to feel the presence of legions of angels passing through our forms and our auras. He reminds us to "Be not forgetful to entertain strangers; for thereby some have entertained angels unawares." [3]

Serapis thanks Justinius, who bows to us and withdraws. And then Serapis continues his instruction.

"*I realize that I have not defined some of the words used in this session, such as* Elohim, fourth ray, violet flame, four lower bodies, hierarchy *and a few others. Please write them in your notebooks and I shall explain at a later date. For now, it is getting late and it is time for us to close tonight. God bless you all in your meditations and communion with these heavenly hosts.*"

We are all somewhat relieved, for although we have been blessed by so much transcendent information, we can't wait to get home and digest what we have received. We need some time to meditate and to process all this. We want to be careful that we don't lose a single drop of these beautiful teachings. And we certainly want time to look over our notes and get to know El Morya, Saint Germain, Justinius and his seraphim.

∾If you wish to further enhance your study before proceeding to Chapter 4, you will find exercises on p. 221.

❧

CHAPTER FOUR

The Ascension Is an Initiation

As the master approaches the platform to give us our next lesson, we look around and see that tonight we are seated in a large amphitheater. Rows and rows of bleachers form a semicircle behind us, or so it seems. They are filled with young souls who have been invited to attend the next few lectures on the initiations of the ascension. The Master Serapis begins speaking immediately:

"The ascension is an initiation, in fact the final initiation, on the path that leads home to God. In future classes we will discuss the steps to the ascension, but for now, remember that I have said, 'You ascend daily. Initiations cannot be taken all at once. They are taken over the spiral of not one lifetime but many lifetimes.'"

We realize that we must have passed many initiations already or we would not be attending this series of lectures at the Ascension Temple. Nonetheless, we may have failed some initiations and therefore need to take them over again. We may have even refused them when they were first presented to us.

Serapis Bey is a no nonsense master who gives us all the information we need. He continues to instruct us from the Dossier on the Ascension:

"You cannot produce the necessary change in consciousness that will fit you for our cosmic band unless there is a willingness on your part to relinquish ties to human foolishness. If you would wait a million years for mastery, go find another. For Serapis is impatient for perfection.

"Men require spunk and a straight spine. There is no question that they have pampered themselves, and that with illusion. Straight talk and straight thought will do much to *clear the way; and it will not place any individual outside the citadel of hope, but wholly within it. My motto is, 'The disciplines of life must be inflexible. Otherwise there can be no discipline.'*

"The ascension must be desired and it must be desired ordinately. It must not be desired as a mechanism of escape from responsibility or from worldly duties. It must be desired as the culmination of a lifetime of service in the will of God. Men must be willing during their final embodiments upon the planet—the time of their escape from the round of the centuries—to give the very best of service to the light and to help usher in the kingdom.

"The way of escape for every man is the path of the ascension and this is the gift of God to each one, whether men realize it or not." [1]

We sit silently as we assimilate Serapis' words and continue to reflect on their implications.

The Initiation of the Ascension

Serapis has emphasized that immortality comes at a high price and it demands the allness of men from the smallness of men. Men cannot build out of mortal substance immortal bodies. They cannot build out of mortal feelings divine feelings that enfold the world and create the great Pyramid of Life.

None of our teachers in school taught us about the path to the ascension, nor did they tell us that it is God's greatest gift to us. And yet I think I must have always had a soul awareness of it, for I always knew that there must be something more to life than our everyday existence.

Now that I am aware of the gift of the ascension, I am determined to dedicate my life to telling as many people as I can about this great dispensation of grace. In informal talks with students, I have found that most of them feel the same way. Look out world, here we come!

However, we have millions of ways of explaining our actions

when we do not want to pass an initiation. We claim the right to do our own thing by performing good works on this planet and justifying our actions by saying that we are doing this for God. But we really need God's representatives, the ascended masters and their messenger, the embodied guru, to help us safely and quickly climb the pyramid of the ascension. El Morya has said that "the Path is strewn with the bleached bones of solitary climbers."

We may have meandered through many a lifetime, refusing an initiation that came directly from a master, even perhaps without recognizing it. We may have veered off in many directions and become involved in other paths—the psychic world, probes into flying saucers or clairvoyance. Many became do-gooders and justified their existence on this basis.

All these things are sidetracks for souls who may have chosen to refuse the basic initiations that probably involved the surrender of pride and the surrender of the ego. And so we rationalized our own little path as we became feverishly involved in this or that endeavor.

Climbing the Pyramid of the Ascension

Let's look at a concept of the ascension that Serapis has given us to meditate on—the concept of climbing the pyramid of the ascension.

We are attempting to leave footprints in the sands of time for others to follow, for we are all climbing the pyramid of the ascension. Pyramids are made up of steps and although we may see just an equilateral triangle when we look at a pyramid, it is really made of large blocks of stone that form individual steps.

In Mexico and Yucatan we can spend days climbing the ruins of the pyramids, each step taking us nearer the top. But the pyramid we are climbing today is not one of stone, it is the pyramid of our ascension. Our thoughts, our feelings, our actions are all steps we are taking on the way up to the apex of this pyramid. For we do not ascend all at once, we ascend daily.

From a distance, the pyramids in Yucatan and the Great

Pyramid of Giza in Egypt seem to be smooth, symmetrical tri-angles. It is only on closer inspection that we notice that some of the steps are broken, weathered or even missing. We can medi-tate on how our lives parallel these triangles with their beauty and their rough spots.

Our lives do not always form a constantly ascending spiral, for we do not always keep progressing steadily up the pyramid. Sometimes we have to stop to get our breath or we may actually stumble and slide down a step or two.

The Ebb and Flow of Life

At times we will be in the ebb of life, when we feel that we are not progressing, when we feel that all the world is arrayed against us and we are of little value. These are the times when we need to rest secure in God's arms, knowing that we are a son or daughter of God and that he is our true Father. It is time to rest and pour out our love to him.

Life is cyclic. Think of the ocean waves. Never does a wave go out that does not come back in. Have you ever seen the water go out and out and out, and remain out? When you feel dis-couraged, think of the ocean. As the tide turns, your life may turn around also. Send your love to God and rest in full assurance that by the law of life, what you give out must come back to you, magnified ten times or more. Know that on the next flow, the next crest, you will come up slightly higher than you were before.

When we make mistakes, it is important that we get up and go on and do not spend time criticizing ourselves for our failures. El Morya teaches: "Do not, then, decry the fact that you must of necessity make some mistakes. Do not remain upon the ground when you fall or stumble. Arise at once and proceed onward."

He encourages us by reminding us that "the trek upward is worth the inconvenience." And Saint Germain also admonishes us to be sure to get up one more time than we fall.

We should analyze ourselves, but not in a spirit of self-condemnation or belittlement. For by God's grace, we will be one step higher on the pyramid next time around. We may also call to him for forgiveness saying, "Father, here I am; I didn't do everything that I had planned, but, beloved Saint Germain, in the name of my I AM Presence, I ask for another chance. Please transmute today's mistakes and all my errors of the past by the mercy of your violet flame and may I go forward again as a son or daughter of God."

At this moment we notice a slight interruption in the back of the room. Someone has raised a hand. "Please excuse me, beloved master, but I can't contain my excitement any longer. What is the violet flame? How do I use it to transmute my errors of the past? This sounds like just the answer I have been looking for."

Serapis smiles at his enthusiasm and notices that many of us are also eager for the same instruction. But he replies, "Let's take a short break now, and I'll call the Ascended Master Saint Germain to join us. I had planned on having one entire class on the violet flame, but perhaps Saint Germain will agree to give us a little preliminary glimpse of his great gift to the world."

During our break we remind each other of what we have learned about Saint Germain in an earlier class. Calling us to order, Serapis announces, "I would like you to meet the Ascended Master Saint Germain, Lord of the Seventh Ray and the Master of Aquarius."

Saint Germain enters, dressed in a luminous violet robe. We can all feel the pulsations of his purple, fiery heart.

Violet Flame in the Retreats

Saint Germain has told us that the violet flame is the flame of the Aquarian Age; it is the color of freedom itself.

The violet flame has always been used in the etheric retreats of the Great White Brotherhood. There the masters receive only the most worthy chelas for instruction on the path of initiation. Thus the violet flame was reserved for the privileged few until the time in this century when Saint Germain went before the Lords of Karma and received permission to make it available to all.

No longer is it necessary to spend one's entire life traveling at great physical peril to the mystery schools of the Brotherhood located in inaccessible reaches of the Himalayas or in India, China or Egypt. Now, in the comfort of our own home or sanctuary, we can invoke this sacred-fire aspect of the Holy Spirit and receive from it great benefits of healing and freedom.

During the old occult, or hidden, dispensation, many of the truths of the Brotherhood were kept from the eyes of the world. We are living in a time when the dispensation has been given to Saint Germain to disseminate this knowledge freely to all who will receive it and use it for their freedom and for the freedom of the planet.

Serapis Bey turns to Saint Germain and says, "Will you please enlighten us, beloved Saint Germain?"

Saint Germain nods and we turn to him in eager anticipation of his words:

"The dispensation of the violet flame is a revelation of light that will allow all that is not right on earth to be righted by the law of freedom and by that baptism of the sacred fire.

"Understand, then, that it is movement to the great God Self within you that is your salvation in this age. All problems of the economy, the ecology and the government can be resolved if you will take only ten minutes each day to go within and find your own God Self, to meditate and to use the science of the spoken Word whereby you chant the mantra of the free: I AM a being of violet fire! I AM the purity God desires!

"This is my mantra which I give to you as your initiation into the Aquarian age.

"When you use the name of God to claim the I AM as God's being and be-ness within you, then you have that claim to all which follows. And therefore you can take the mantra of Jesus Christ, 'I AM the way, the truth and the life,'² and you may participate in that glorious life that he lived."³

Saint Germain's Violet Flame

Saint Germain is offering us his Aquarian-age mantra for our own use. We can allow this mantra to sing through our minds whenever we have a few minutes—when we are waiting for the traffic light to change, when we are waiting in the doctor's office for an appointment or waiting for someone to answer the phone.

I AM a being of violet fire! I AM the purity God desires!

If you would have the benefit of this miraculous energy, you have only to make the call, for the call compels the answer. Accept this gift of the violet flame on faith; and if you do not actually see it, don't let it worry you in the least. Many people do not. Just try to imagine how it would feel penetrating your pores, coming down as a ray from God, from your I AM Presence, coming down through the crystal cord. See it come down to the threefold flame in your heart.

See this ray of violet hit the earth and spring up as a beautiful flame. See the violet flame coming up from the earth. Don't just see it coming from above where your Higher Body is. See it also sweeping below where your problems are. If you can't see it, just feel it. If you can't feel it, just use your imagination.

Saint Germain suggests that to help our visualization we may wish to buy a piece of violet satin or velvet and place it on our altar so that we can physically see the color of violet as we decree.

Through the spectrum, violet extends from deep purple, including much of the blue of the will of God, to an almost pink-violet that is the mercy flame containing the love of God. As you decree, see the violet flame changing from deep purple to lavender to pink-violet.

You may want to visualize whatever is wrong in your world being whirled about as if in a giant centrifuge, and then see all that you would be rid of just disappearing up in smoke. This beautiful, blazing, singing flame of mercy and transmutation is truly the wine of forgiveness, the wine of the Holy Spirit.

The way to get rid of psychological problems, hang-ups, depressions or records of the past is to visualize ourselves standing in a sphere of violet light, feeling the violet flame passing through our consciousness, our mind, our feelings, our emotions. There is no need to go through hypnosis or regression, for when we call upon this action of the Holy Spirit, all our fears, hatreds, resentments and rebellions are dissolved in the flame, and our consciousness is restored to the clarity of the Christ mind.

Always remember that exposure to the divine flames can never harm or alter any part of your being that is already perfected. Just as those who are wise seek to purge their bodies as well as their emotions from unwanted substance, so it is essential that they purify their entire consciousness by calling into action the blessed violet flame, which focuses the forgiving, transmuting power of God.

Saint Germain assures us that all that the masters require of us is our hearts and voices uplifted to give these invocations. Only by decree and prayer can heaven enter earth, and Saint Germain tells us solemnly that deliverance will not come unless it be invoked! God cannot act except through us.

The flame of transmutation must be invoked daily if we are to effectively dissolve our ancient records of error. It is important that we not let a day go by without calling for the flame to be reanchored in our world; for if it is not invoked once every twenty-four hours, the flame has a tendency to rise again to its home in the octaves of light.

Serapis says he would like to give us one important bit of instruction which he included in his Dossier on the Ascension:

"In order to ascend you must abandon your past to God, knowing that he possesses the power, by his flame and identity, to change all that you have wrought by malintent and confusion into the beauty of the original design. Possess the willingness, in the name of Almighty God, to change your world!"[4]

Abandon Your Past to God

It is not always easy to let go of our past, but it is in our best interest to abandon it to God, for he has the ability to transform it. It seems that many hang on desperately to the past, saying, "Well, such-and-such didn't happen and such-and-such did happen, therefore, it makes me the way I am." But remember, as the master said, in order to ascend you must abandon your past to God.

Every time painful incidents of the past come into your mind, throw them back into the flame. And pretty soon that memory won't be so vivid. It will become duller and duller and eventually you can completely clear it from your mind.

Saint Germain released the music of the flame of freedom a century ago in Europe in the three-quarter time of the Johann Strauss waltzes. So put on a recording of the "Blue Danube," the "Emperor's Waltz," or "Tales of the Vienna Woods," and, as El Morya says, "Let your house be a house of light! Let your aura be filled with the joyous fires of freedom! Roll out the violet carpet and see how the masters will come to teach you and to lead you in the paths of righteousness for His name's sake."

Saint Germain, having completed his remarks for the evening, is ready to leave. But first he issues us a challenge!

"You'll never know until you TRY! You can make it if you TRY! The way to spell try is capital T, capital R, capital Y—You can make it if you TRY.

"Here is the sacred formula: Theos=God; Rule=Law; You=Being; Theos + Rule + You = God's Law active as Principle within your being (TRY)." [5]

After Saint Germain exits, one young man vows to himself that he will print a little card that says "I can make it if I TRY," and put it on his computer screen. The lady next to him chuckles as she overhears his plan, for she has just such a card on her bathroom mirror where she can see it readily. Both of them agree that the next step is to accept the help that Saint Germain is so generously offering.

∽ *If you wish to further enhance your study before proceeding to Chapter 5, you will find exercises on p. 222.*

🌿

CHAPTER FIVE

Requirements
for the Ascension

The ritual of the ascension is the goal for every lifestream who understands his reason for being," Serapis tells us. "This initiation can and will come to anyone—even a little child when he is ready.

"There are several requirements. I will list each one and then discuss them in more detail later. To make your ascension you must:

- Balance your Threefold Flame
- Align your four lower bodies
- Attain a balance of mastery on all seven rays
- Achieve mastery over outer conditions
- Fulfill your divine plan
- Transmute your electronic belt
- Raise the sacred fire from the base of the spine to the crown
- Balance 51 percent of your karma

I would like to invite Saint Germain to take over the class now and explain the first requirement to balance the threefold flame."

Balance the Threefold Flame

Saint Germain rises and begins to address us.

"Thank you for this opportunity. The study of the three-fold flame is very close to my heart. This is the flame of the Christ that is anchored in the secret chamber of the heart and contains three plumes—the sacred trinity of blue for the power of God, yellow for the wisdom of God and pink for the love of God.

"*Within the heart there is a central chamber surrounded by a forcefield of such light and protection that we call it a 'cosmic interval.' It is a chamber separated from matter, and no probing could ever discover it. It occupies simultaneously not only the third and fourth dimensions but also other dimensions unknown to man.*

"*Each acknowledgment paid daily to the flame within your heart will amplify the power and illumination of love within your being. It is your personal focus of the sacred fire. It is your point of contact with the Divine; a spark of fire from the Creator's own heart. It is your opportunity to become the Christ; it is the potential of your Divinity waiting to burst into being within your humanity.*

"*The balance of the threefold flame creates a pattern of the ascension for all. Imbalance—where gigantism occurs in one aspect of the threefold flame, causing it to be out of proportion to the others—prevents the achievement of daily goals as well as the goal of individual Christ-mastery. With each increase of wisdom, the power and love plumes must also rise by the fiat of your devotion to goodwill, else wisdom's gain will not be retained. Likewise, with each getting of power, there must come the attainment of wisdom and love in perfect complement; so, too, love is actualized only through an equivalency of power and wisdom.*"[1]

How to Balance the Threefold Flame

Recognizing that balance is the golden key to Christhood, I want to point out to you that if you want to develop the flame within your heart, you cannot become a one-sided individual who loves intellectual pursuits to the extent that you withdraw into an ivory tower and ignore your responsibilities to your city and nation and the many unfortunates who need your love and caring. The same holds true if you are just a sweet, loving person who refuses to take responsibility or to pursue the path of learning.

What we call a blue-ray person, one in whose aura the blue

plume is dominant, must remember to balance power with illumination and love. El Morya has told us that the true blue-ray man derives his power from dipping deeply into the reservoir of love within his heart.

Progress stems, then, from attunement with these three aspects of God in perfect balance. Every individual threefold flame is different just as every Causal Body is different. It is the same threefold flame, but its power, its energy, its identity, its size and whether or not it is balanced depends upon your individualization of that flame.

Each time you pass a test, you are balancing and increasing your threefold flame. And so each test that is passed successfully gives you a greater momentum of the Christ consciousness to apply to the next initiation.

At the conclusion of this instruction, Saint Germain takes a moment to relate an incident that occurred when heart transplants first became possible. One of his students was new to the teachings and quite perturbed as to the consequences of a heart transplant, should she ever require one. She phoned Mark Prophet, her Guru, and asked him whose threefold flame she would have then, her own or the donor's? She was quite concerned about it.

Mark assured her that her threefold flame would remain safely intact in the secret chamber of her heart, a spiritual place separate from her physical heart. He said that if she ever needed a transplant to maintain her life, she should go right ahead and have one; her threefold flame would still be her own.

Saint Germain says that he is relating this incident in case anyone else in the class might have a similar question.

Saint Germain turns to Serapis and says, "Thank you for allowing me to speak to your students. Perhaps you would like to take over now and discuss the rest of the requirements for the ascension."

Serapis explains that the next topic will be the alignment of the four lower bodies.

Align the Four Lower Bodies

The four lower bodies must be aligned to function as chalices for God's light. These bodies may be described as four sheaths—etheric, mental, emotional and physical—surrounding the soul and vibrating at different frequencies.

The etheric, or memory body, is the vehicle for the soul and holds the blueprint of the perfect image to be portrayed in the world of form. As the only permanent body, it is carried over from one lifetime to the next, whereas the mental, emotional and physical bodies go through the process of disintegration after death.

The higher etheric body is designed to anchor in man the perfection of his God Presence and the divine blueprint of his individuality. The lower etheric body contains his subconscious mind and stores all his experiences—all the thoughts, feelings, words and actions that were ever expressed through the other three bodies.

The mental body was designed to contain the mind of God, but today we have a buildup of many false concepts because of the bombardment of the media—movies, television and books—and unfortunately it is sometimes easier for our worldly mind to replace the mind of Christ. Often we lower our standards without realizing it because of society's influence on us through what we allow into our lives.

The emotional body is our feeling body, sometimes called the desire body or the astral body. Often our feelings, desires and emotions are more turbulent than peaceful. Lunar influences can also affect this body, especially during the time of the full moon.

However, we can and must take command of our emotions if our goal is the ascension. Jesus' simple command, "Peace, be still!"[2] can instantly bring our emotions under control if we are constantly on guard against them and are aware of any mounting agitation.

Often our concern centers on our physical body but misuses of the other bodies, even in past lifetimes, can result in the diseases that arise in our physical body today. As the Buddhists say, we are fortunate to have a body, and so it is in our best interest to take good care of ourselves and eat healthful foods, exercise, fast occasionally, get the proper rest, and so forth.

Many souls are waiting at the portals of birth, just begging for a chance to be given a body. Millions of souls who were granted one have been aborted and have thus lost their opportunity this time around. Abortion is a great crime that has prevented many souls from fulfilling their divine plan and our hearts go out to these aborted babies, many of whom are old souls destined to play a part in the coming age of Aquarius.

Our four lower bodies are really four energy fields, four interpenetrating sheaths of consciousness, each vibrating in its own dimension. These bodies surround the soul and are its vehicles of expression in the world of form. They are intended to function as an integrated unit, somewhat like wheels within wheels.

The easiest way for us to visualize this is to think of them as interpenetrating colanders. When the "holes" are lined up, your four bodies are in sync and thus the light can flow through the chakras without obstruction. However, most of us don't have our holes lined up and so we are out of alignment with our Real Self, our Christ Self. Thus the requirement for the ascension is that our four lower bodies be aligned and functioning as receptacles for God's light.

In addition to the four lower bodies, we have three higher bodies, for man is a sevenfold being. The three higher bodies are:

- The I AM Presence, also known as the God Presence, is God individualized for each one of us.
- The Causal Body, the color rings that surround the I AM Presence, contains man's "treasure in heaven." [3]
- The Christ Self, the Mediator between God and man, is sometimes referred to as the Higher Mental Body. It overshadows all the four lower bodies.

Mastery on All Seven Rays

The next requirement for the ascension is to attain a balance of mastery on all seven rays. You may have lived several consecutive lifetimes on the same ray but by the time you are ready for your ascension you will have lived many, many times on all seven rays, and should have developed a rainbow aura.

"*And now,*" Serapis Bey says, "*many of you have waited for me to explain the rays. I gave you a few hints when I referred to El Morya as a first-ray man and Saint Germain as a seventh-ray master. Let's take a moment and think about the color rays that descend from the heart of the sun.*"

- *The first ray is blue and is the ray of the will of God.*
- *The second ray is yellow and personifies wisdom and illumination.*
- *The third ray is pink and is the ray of Divine Love.*
- *The fourth ray is white and is the ray of purity and the ascension.*
- *The fifth ray is green and is the ray of truth, science and healing.*
- *The sixth ray, purple and gold with ruby flecks, is the ray of ministration and service.*
- *And the seventh, or violet, ray is the ray of mercy, freedom and transmutation.*

Although you undoubtedly have greater mastery on one or more of these rays, you will need balance on all seven rays for your ascension. As you progress in your understanding of the teachings of the ascended masters, you often begin to feel an affinity for one of the rays and a special closeness to the master who is your Guru.

Mastery over Outer Conditions

The next requirement for the ascension is for the candidate to have attained mastery over every outer condition. Such mastery implies that the disciple is able to rise above the suffering of sin, sickness and death and retain his harmony through all the tests and trials that come to him.

We should understand by that that we do not have to be in the peak of health to ascend. In fact, that is seldom the case. But people in the throes of a terminal illness may have risen above their pain and at the same time may also be praising God. In this way, they are gaining their mastery over sin, sickness and death.

Fulfill One's Divine Plan

The fulfillment of one's divine plan is a further requirement for the ascension. One of the reasons a soul might need to reembody is if his divine plan requires that he come to earth again for a special mission that only he can perform. Any decision on this would be made in agreement with his Holy Christ Self and the Karmic Board.

Transmute the Electronic Belt

The next requirement is the transmutation of the electronic belt, or the residue of our karma. Called the subconscious and unconscious minds by psychologists, this so-called belt is positioned in the person's aura around the lower part of the form. It extends from the waist to beneath the feet somewhat in the shape of a large kettledrum and contains the records of our negative thoughts and feelings.

This kettledrum of negative energy can be clearly seen by those who have clairvoyant vision. It is filled with hard, dense material that has accumulated over thousands of years. We must transmute it by the violet flame and by our service to the world. And when we do, the resulting purified substance can be raised and stored in our Causal Body.

It is time to transcend our cycles and to no longer repeat those negative spirals over and over again. With one invocation to the ascension fire, we can let that flame leap and arc from spiral to spiral, consuming the debris on contact. And then our soul, enveloped in the flame, need not remain any longer in that consciousness. Serapis says, "Transcend it!"

Raise the Light from the Base of the Spine to the Crown

The raising of the light from the base of the spine to the crown of the head, called the raising of the Kundalini in the East, is another requirement for the ascension. It involves the lifting of the energy lying dormant in the base-of-the-spine chakra up the spinal altar and through the chakras to the crown. This is a very important process that can be dangerous if the light rises before the chakras are purified by the violet flame.

The masters do not recommend the practice of Kundalini yoga to raise this energy prematurely. Serious physical consequences can result, even insanity, if "heaven suffereth violence." [4] The practice of giving the violet flame daily will allow the Kundalini energy to rise gently and safely.

Balance 51 Percent of Your Karma

In earlier ages, we were required to balance 100 percent of our karma before we could return to the heart of God. Every jot and tittle[5] of the law had to be fulfilled; every erg of energy misqualified throughout all our incarnations had to be purified before we could ascend. Perfection was the requirement of the law.

Now, thanks to the mercy of God and the Lords of Karma, the old law has been set aside and those who have balanced only 51 percent of their debts to life can be given the gift of the ascension. They can then balance the remaining 49 percent from the ascended realm through service to earth and her evolutions.

We receive increments of light daily, and all of nature must adjust to this influx of light. Often our physical bodies go through difficult adjustments to the new light given to us. As our bodies cannot contain darkness and light at the same time, sometimes the process of flushing out the darkness is rather uncomfortable. This may account for those days when we just don't feel well and yet have no recognizable illness.

One Ascension Per Year Requirement

As long as some are willing to submit to the disciplines of the master of the Ascension Temple, the world will remain a place of opportunity for evolving souls. And as long as at least one ascension takes place each year, we will see progress in human evolution.

When earth passed through the dark ages, years went by

when only one soul was able to meet the requirements of the ascension. Yet because of that one soul, God allows us to keep our planet as a platform for evolution if one soul ascends yearly.

During other periods of great enlightenment and progress, many souls have ascended each year. Science, invention, education, the fields of medicine and healing are quickened and propelled forward by the action of the ascension of these souls. And so progress on the planet is in direct proportion to the evolution of individual souls.

The process of the ascension is not an illusory event; it is actually happening today. There have been ages when the ascended masters were not allowed to contact people in embodiment as they do at present. But we live in an age of enlightenment when the ascended masters can teach those who are receptive. The masters have prophesied that there will be mass ascensions from the hillsides in the golden age of Aquarius.

As we conclude this session, Serapis Bey smiles and says, "And now, dear hearts, did you like tonight's lesson? I hope you all took good notes, because you realize that it is necessary for me to test you just as in any university in the world. I must ascertain just how much your soul retains and internalizes of the material presented. And, of course, your ascension in the light will be the proof that you have passed the course!

"Remember that El Morya said, 'The trek upward is worth the inconvenience.' And this is true indeed. Good night, dear souls of my heart."

꙳ If you wish to further enhance your study before proceeding to Chapter 6, you will find exercises on p. 222.

❦

CHAPTER SIX

Physical Changes in the Ascension

Serapis Bey and Saint Germain both greet us tonight and tell us that they will be sharing in the presentation. Serapis says, "I have sensed your eagerness to know exactly what physical changes will occur when you ascend. But you have been too polite to interrupt the flow of the teachings. I am glad to see that you have contained your impatience until now.

"Tonight we have a treat in store for you. We are going to show you the ascension process as it happens on inner planes. And I will describe it using the words of Jesus' disciple John the Beloved who experienced his ascension at the conclusion of his Palestinian lifetime."

John the Beloved begins to speak to us: "How can we convey to those of you who have not experienced the influx of the great current of the ascension spiral what this energy is? Shall we say that it is like the splitting of a thousand or ten thousand atoms with man himself being in the center? Shall we say that it is like the explosion of worlds and sun-centers? Or shall we say that it is like the unfolding of a lily or a rose?

"Perhaps the poetry of the ascension ought to be written by yourself as you experience that great ritual—perhaps at the close of this life. For, as you have been taught, the doors are open to all who will make the call and give the service and apply for the test.

"Line upon line, precept upon precept, the victory is won. You are ascending daily. You are ascending in spirals of your own being, your own consciousness. You are not as you were yesterday or last week. And if you are giving daily devotions to the Most High, you are light-years beyond your former self years ago."

At this point, Saint Germain takes the lectern:

"*When the gift of the ascension is given to anyone by his own I AM Presence and the Karmic Board, the appearance of age drops from him as swiftly as a smile can raise the lips. The magnetism and energy of that one become the unlimited power of God, pulsing through his being.*

"*The dross of the physical body, the weariness of the emotional body, tired of the creations of hatred, the ceaseless rote of the mental body—all drop away and are replaced in perfect ease by their divine counterparts. The feelings become charged by the love of God and the angels. The mind is imbued with the diamond-shining Mind of God—omnipresent, omniscient and omnipotent. The total being is inspired and aspiring!*"[1]

The Ascension

Serapis will now teach us from the *Dossier on the Ascension*:

"Although the form of an individual may show signs of age prior to his ascension, all of this will change and the physical appearance of the individual will be transformed into the glorified body. The individual ascends then, not in an earthly body but in a glorified spiritual body into which the physical form is changed on the instant by total immersion in the great God flame.

"Thus man's consciousness of the physical body ceases and he achieves a state of weightlessness. This resurrection takes place as the great God flame envelops the remaining shell of human creation that remains and transmutes, in a pattern of cosmic grids, all of the cell patterns of the individual—the bony structure, the blood vessels and all bodily processes go through a great metamorphosis.

"The blood in the veins changes to liquid golden light; the throat chakra glows with an intense blue-white light; the spiritual eye in the center of the forehead becomes an elongated God-flame rising upwards. The garments of the individual are completely consumed and he takes on the appearance of being clothed in a white robe, the seamless garment of the Christ. Sometimes the long hair of the Higher Mental Body (the Christ Self) appears as pure gold on the ascending one; then again, eyes of any color may become a beautiful electric blue or a pale violet.

"These changes are permanent. The ascended one is able to take his light body with him wherever he wishes, or he may travel without the glorified spiritual body. Ascended beings can, and occasionally do, appear upon earth as ordinary mortals, putting on physical garments resembling those of the people of earth and moving among them for cosmic purposes. This Saint Germain did after his ascension when he was known as the Wonderman of Europe. Such an activity is a matter of dispensation received from the Karmic Board." [2]

We must add, however, that ascended beings do not generally return to earth unless there is some special need for them to do so. We have seen how in a moment, in the twinkling of an eye, the ascending one is changed. His flesh becomes transparent. His veins are filled with golden-pink light. The very atoms of his being become lighter.

The ascension is a raising action that affects the entire being of man. In this weightless condition man's buoyant, God-free form can no longer be bound to earth. His body grows lighter and lighter and with the weightlessness of helium begins to rise into the atmosphere as the gravitational pull is loosened.

Through this process the son becomes one with the Father. He can no longer remain tied to the earth, for he is filled with the light of the Sun and he has no further need for a body. Like Jesus he rises "into the air" where a cloud of white light receives him out of sight and he is once again united with the Father, the I AM Presence. This is the glory of the ascension process that Jesus demonstrated for us.

Serapis tells us that we will discuss in our next meeting how some who have earned their ascension on occasion volunteer to surrender this blessing in order to assist those who are still in the process of overcoming. In Buddhism, they are called bodhisattvas. In the mountains of the Himalayas, some unascended ascended masters have volunteered to remain with the evolutions of earth until every last man, woman and child is free in the ascension. However, this is a rare occurrence, and in the West we are encouraged to take our ascension when it is offered to us, both for our own benefit and that of the planet.

Remember that we have been admonished that one of the demands of the Lords of Karma is that at least one individual graduate each year to renew the grant of light that is necessary to maintain the stability of the planet.

The Ascension Retreat

A final word, now, about the Ascension Temple. In addition to the spiritual focus at Luxor, the ruins of a great temple remain there. Candidates for the ascension may come to this Ascension Temple at the conclusion of their life to receive the initiation that will reunite them with their God Presence.

Accompanied by ascended and unascended masters, the candidate is bidden by the master of the retreat to stand in the center of the ascension flame. At that point the individual's cosmic tone is sounded and the flame from Alpha is released from above and the flame from Omega rises from below.

When the individual's tone is sounded and the flame is released, the seraphim in the outer court trumpet the victory of the ascending soul with a magnificent rendition of the "Triumphal March" from *Aïda*. The discipline that is the keynote of this retreat is felt in their precise, golden-tone rendition of the piece.

It is the march of your victory! Each time you hear those trumpets you can know that it commemorates the moment when you will step onto the dais in the center of the Ascension Temple. With the seraphim surrounding the dais, and all the brothers and sisters of the Ascension Temple encircling you, you will rise in the ritual of the ascension—**an Ascended Master! Immortal!**

With a silent blessing the masters withdraw, enabling us to meditate upon the glorious truths we have received and the present possibility of our own ascension.

᠅ *If you wish to further enhance your study before proceeding to Chapter 7, you will find exercises on p. 223.*

🦋

CHAPTER SEVEN

I AM My Brother's Keeper

Serapis Bey takes his place at the lectern again and says, "After that transcendent experience last night, let's return to the task at hand and continue climbing the pyramid of the ascension. You remember that we interrupted our climb to discuss the violet flame. And so, onward!"

It Is Not Selfish to Ascend

A moment comes in the life of every initiate when he must answer the question: "Am I my brother's keeper?"[1] The answer is yes. For although it is true that the master wants you to ascend, he also wants you to bring your brother with you.

He wants you to pray for the rest of the world and balance part of your karma through service. And if you can do more good with another embodiment, I'm sure your soul and your Christ Self would be happy to say, "Fine, I'll come back."

Never fear that it is selfish to make your ascension. On the other hand, don't pursue your ascension to the exclusion of service to your fellowman. Many individuals are so involved in the battle of winning their ascension that they completely ignore their responsibilities to their fellowman and to hierarchy. And so here again we must answer the question of whether we are our brother's keeper with the same answer, yes.

It is not selfish of us to take our ascension, because as each one ascends, part of the light released is given back to earth. Each ascending one raises the earth and all mankind a little. We are all on a spiral; others are coming up behind us on the steps, and as we move on into the ascended realm, they follow us and also move up.

One of the demands of the Lords of Karma is that a certain number graduate each year to renew the grant of light necessary to maintain the thrust of the planet. So even though we may think that because of the conditions in the world we could help the Brotherhood more by forgoing our ascension, the masters need many to ascend at the end of the age of Pisces.

Jesus, the Master of the Piscean Age, came to set the example for us and we have had two thousand years to become as he was, or put on our Christhood as he did. For many of us, this is meant to be our last embodiment and our next assignment will be to continue our service from the ascended realm.

As each soul ascends, an increment of light is anchored on earth; therefore our ascension can benefit the planetary body as well as everyone on earth. Each individual's victory contributes to the victory of the whole human race.

Climbing the Peaks of the Himalayas

When we realize that we have received an understanding given to few on the planet, then we must also understand that because of this knowledge we hold the light for millions. And if we let go of the light, it's as though we were at the head of a group of climbers on a peak in the Himalayas and we let go of the rope that binds them all together. All the climbers behind us depend on us and the rope. If we let that rope fall, everybody falls.

If we actually were climbing that mountain, we wouldn't be so willing to let go of the rope. We wouldn't allow any lethargy or distraction or any pleasure of the senses to take us from our post and cause a thousand or ten thousand souls to fall.

But when the tempter comes in the hours of trial that come to every aspirant, he will tell us that it doesn't matter what we do with our life, for who will know and who will care and who will be affected? The tempter will always say that we can have another chance at our mastery; there's no need to be in a hurry about our ascent.

Have you ever heard those little voices talking to you when you were tired, when you had a cold, when you wanted to do anything rather than pick up your prayer book and give your invocations for the world? And so, in those hours of depression when the dark clouds hover, we forget that there are a million souls who are nourished by our prayers, by our meditations, by our invocations and by our love.

If Jesus, Mother Mary, or any of the ascended masters who sponsor us were suddenly to take their leave of this planet, you would actually have the experience that the one ahead of you had let go of the rope. And you would find yourself tumbling into the abyss of your own sin, of your own karma.

As I meditate on the master's words on karma, I think how sad it is that millions of good souls are not even aware that they have karma to balance. The teachings on karma and reincarnation were removed from the early Church by succeeding church councils, and are not taught today in most churches. It is our assignment today to return Jesus' true teachings to his own.

We saw earlier that there are avatars on the path just slightly ahead of us who are holding back world karma (and perhaps part of our karma) until they see that we are strong enough to bear that karma. Then it is returned to us and perhaps we may take on some karma for others that has been set aside for them, so that they may advance to their Christ-mastery. This is how hierarchy works, and hierarchy is a link to eternity.

Another aspect that we have not discussed is that there are others behind us who are waiting for us to move on—to leave the step we're standing on. They are waiting for us to go up higher so that they can move to the step we have just left. By refusing our initiations, we are holding others back.

Serapis Bey teaches that the ascended masters realize that failures will occur. But they want us to understand—today and forever—that failures are only a momentary falling short of a momentary mark.

El Morya has told us many times, "From the beginning we were winning." It is with our ultimate victories that we are concerned, not with the skirmishes that are lost or won each hour and each day.

The Advantage of Being Alive Today

We have the distinct advantage of being alive today, the masters tell us, for we can work out our karma quickly and satisfactorily. Only a certain part of karma can be balanced after we ascend. No matter how well we may know the law or how much we may have studied at night when we were out of the body or between embodiments, we still must return to this world to prove our mastery of that law.

Here is where we made our mistakes, so here is where we must correct them. The master says that we are indeed fortunate to have a twofold action—the advantage of the masters' teachings and a body in which to work out our karma. When we are in the etheric retreats between lifetimes, we cannot balance the karma we made with people on earth. As much as possible, it must be done in interaction with those with whom we made it, and so we keep returning.

We need to transmute the wrongs of this lifetime with violet flame. And when we come this near to the end of the Path, this near the top of the pyramid of the ascension, we are also responsible for all the energy that we have ever misqualified back to our earliest embodiment. It is all coming up now for redemption, and we have to balance at least 51 percent of it.

Serapis has explained the law to us in banking terms: We may take out a loan for a thousand dollars that only requires us to pay ten dollars a month, but at the end of three years, the entire balance is due all at once as a balloon payment.

When we were not strong enough to balance all our karma ourselves, in divine mercy by the law of containment it was set aside. But now it is payable on demand just like a note at the bank.

Now is the time to transmute our misuse of God's energy back to our earliest embodiment. And when 51 percent is paid back and we have fulfilled the other requirements that we learned in our earlier lessons, we are assured the prize of the ascension.

Our Example Is Important

Do you remember the little motto we knew as a child, "What you do speaks so loudly that I can't hear what you say?" In the same way we have been told that one who provides a good example is more important to hierarchy than one who may only speak well. The masters feel that initiates must be examples to others so that those who contact us can see that we have something to offer.

Rather than just reading books about the teachings of the ascended masters, we must live them until we become this path and others see the light in us. Then they will want the masters' teachings because of what they see in us. Those who are called to represent hierarchy have been preparing for many centuries for this lifetime.

Serapis Bey says that there is one more important concept that we must learn before we leave tonight—the vow of the bodhisattva.

What Is a Bodhisattva?

One of several definitions of the word bodhisattva that is widely accepted is that a bodhisattva is a being of *bodhi*, or wisdom, who is becoming a Buddha. Another definition, especially in the East, is that a bodhisattva is one who vows to help all sentient beings attain enlightenment.

We see a bodhisattva as one who has earned his ascension but who has renounced the ultimate union with God to bring divine illumination and understanding to his fellowman. He may forgo his reward of the ascension for thousands of years or until every last soul on earth wins her victory.

A bodhisattva may also take his ascension, as the well-known Bodhisattva of the East, Kuan Yin, did and continue to serve the evolutions of earth from the ascended state rather than going on to cosmic service when it is offered. At the present moment, this is the preferred choice.

Kuan Yin is loved in both East and West as the Goddess of Mercy. She has told us that a person on the path of initiation must become a juggler—juggling his own karma, transmuting his mis-qualified energy from past lifetimes and putting it into the flame at the same time as he is putting on the robes of his divinity.

The Bodhisattva Vow

At this moment Serapis waves to Kuan Yin in the hall and invites her to address the students. He says, "Beloved Kuan Yin, I had planned that you would teach on mercy at a future session, for it is a subject with which you are so well acquainted. But now that you are here, will you say a few words?

"I want to be sure that all of our students do not decide to forgo the ascension in order to become bodhisattvas. We need both ascended masters and bodhisattvas in order to hold the light on earth. Or at least, they can take the ascension and still keep their bodhisattva vow from the ascended state as you have."

Kuan Yin points out that the vow taken by the bodhisattva to stand with humanity is a sacred calling, but she cautions us against taking it ourselves unless we thoroughly understand the dedicated service of these ones. She says:

"It is a very high and holy order, and I suggest that you think long and hard about this calling before you respond and say, 'I will do the same.'

"For when aeons pass and men are not moved by the flame that you hold, remember that you might wish you had chosen another easier or more gratifying way.

"As the centuries pass—the thousands of years and the cycles—and the same individuals whom you have nourished by the power of your heart flame are involved in the same involvements in the world, you find that you cry out to God and say, 'O LORD how long! How long will this wayward generation be in coming to the knowledge of the divinity and

the love of the sacred fire that we have held for so long?'"

Serapis thanks Kuan Yin and invites her back whenever she happens to be at the Ascension Temple. "Now," he says, "there is one more office in hierarchy that you need to know about before we close tonight and that is the unascended master."

Unascended Masters

We realize that some great saints and sages (known as unascended masters because they have yet retained their bodies) dwell in the inaccessible reaches of the Himalayas and hold a balance of light for the planet. Seldom do they have contact with civilization in the large cities.

Now that the teachings of the ascended masters have been made known again to devotees, another type of unascended master is added to these great ones who live in the Himalayas and other places of retreat. Today souls who have balanced at least 51 percent of their karma continue to live and work at balancing an even greater amount of their karma while they are able.

From the standpoint of the Master of the Ascension Temple, the solution to the world's problems would be to have more teachers who set forth the teachings of the ascension. Wherever a candidate for the ascension walks upon the earth, he blesses it and all those who contact him.

Thus ascended masters want unascended masters in embodiment. But it's up to you; it's your choice to decide how long it will be before you determine, "Yes, I will be an unascended master, right where I am. I will balance my karma and take dominion over my emotions and be an example to others."

Mankind can only respond to the highest example they see. When they see the light shining on your face, when they feel the love of one who has realized the Presence of God, they will want to experience the teachings of the Great White Brotherhood for themselves. For at first we seek outside ourselves for that which is within.

Serapis closes this evening's session by saying, "Remember, dear hearts, that the ascension is the fulfillment of the will of God for every man. Good evening, candidates for the ascension and those who aspire to be!"

∾ *If you wish to further enhance your study before proceeding to Chapter 8, you will find exercises on p. 224.*

CHAPTER EIGHT

You Are Worthy of Your Ascension

$\mathcal{S}$erapis has told us that if he could only convey one main point to us, it would be to help us to realize that we are worthy of our ascension. Saint Germain has made the promise to you and to me that if we apply ourselves, we can ascend in this life. Or, if there are circumstances that require another incarnation to fulfill our divine plan, we may make our ascension in the next life.

This is the guarantee that has been made to all who diligently pursue the law and the teachings of the ascended masters. For the masters in our midst have given us their unparalleled assistance at the present time.

The ascension is not an intangible something far-off in the distance; it is a real here-and-now possibility. But we have to believe that we can ascend, we have to ask for our ascension and accept it as a gift from God when it is presented to us. Not only is the ascension a reality but it is the purpose of life. We are intended to ascend back to God after victoriously overcoming the world.

But many of us often engage in an activity that is the exact opposite to the flame of purity and self-worth that we should be cultivating. And that's when we run into a serious challenge on the Path that causes a great deal of trouble—self-condemnation.

Self condemnation is insidious and deep-rooted. We can't just tell ourselves to stop indulging in self-condemnation, for stopping this vibration is difficult; in fact, it is one of the most difficult initiations on the path to the ascension.

Self-Condemnation

Quite a stir occurs in the classroom as Serapis escorts the beautiful Goddess of Purity to the lectern. She nods in agreement when Serapis asks her to teach us on the subject of self-condemnation. She begins to speak:

"Gracious ones, so often individuals persist year after year in an attitude of self-condemnation. The way to clear the karmic record is not to engage oneself in this questionable indulgence of reviewing the errors of your lifetime or lifetimes past as snatches of memory come through to your consciousness. Rather, it is the desire of God that you review the great hopeful possibilities of the future.

"There is always the question in the consciousness of those who are prone to repeat the same errors again and again that perhaps God will weary of the number of times they repeat this error. May I point out to you that the eyes of God are too pure to behold iniquity, and the LORD does not suffer from the depredations of men against their own souls. But the suffering and pain is brought out and brought forth to the individual who commits the error.

"The reward for this type of error is no reward at all, but rather brings human pain, mental suffering and criticism of one's own self and often darkens the heart and mind by the concept of impurity. I come, then, this day determined to eradicate those patterns from the mind and consciousness of men.

"While God's purity is not for sale, it is a glad-free gift of his heart to all who yearn for that purity. Purity, precious ones, is a natural quality of God. It is a quality that floods the universe and is responsible for the beautiful pure colors of the rainbow. It is responsible for the clear color of the water when it flows uncontaminated by mortal discord and rubbish.

"So many individuals have spoken to God and in their prayers have said, 'LORD, I am not worthy.' I call to your attention how they are using the power of the I AM to claim unworthiness, when by a simple twist of reversal they could say, correctly so, regardless of the appearances in their consciousness, 'LORD, I am worthy of thy purity.'"

As the Goddess of Purity finishes speaking, we remind ourselves that along with her offer to us comes our responsibility to "go and sin no more."[1]

The choice is ours. We may become depressed and think what terrible sinners we are, or we can realize that we have been given the promise of our ascension. We can have a future of absolute glory if we are willing to start working toward that goal.

Claim Your Purity

Serapis Bey teaches that until you claim the reality of something, you cannot be that reality. So, if you feel that there are still a few areas in your life that have not exactly outpictured the purity that you desire to be, claim that purity! Say, "LORD, I am worthy!" For you are really saying, by using the name I AM, that God in you is worthy of that purity.

You may want to make it a habit, whenever you have a free moment in your day, to claim your victory. Let this mantra echo throughout your consciousness, "I claim my victory now! I claim my victory now! I claim my victory now!" Or if you prefer, "I claim my purity now! I claim my purity now! I claim my purity now!"

You can do this with whatever God-quality you want to increase in yourself. And as you claim it, you are saying that by God's grace, you will be that God-quality in action.

I AM Worthy of Thy Purity

The Goddess of Purity has offered us this prayer that we can make our own.

"LORD, I AM worthy of thy purity. I would have thy purity surge through me in a great cosmic burst to remove from the screen of my mind, my thoughts and my feelings every appearance of human vibratory action and all that is impure in substance, thought or feeling. Replace all that right now with the fullness of the Mind of Christ and the Mind of God, the manifest power of the Resurrection Spirit and the ascension flame, that I may enter into the Holy of holies of my being and find the power of transmutation taking place to free me forever from all discord that has ever manifested in my world."

At the end of the prayer, she continues her teaching:

"I want you, therefore, to understand that while you ought to resist evil, you must understand the need to affirm the power of good and of God's purity far more than you shall engage in an activity of mere resistance. I do not say that there is never a time when you should completely forget about resistance, for the statement and admonishment of the Master, 'Resist the devil and he will flee from you,'[2] is most effective.

"It is simply that you must not spend all of your time fighting or beating the air and forget to establish the patterns of purity which are so essential for you to move forward in the scale of progress. You see, beloved ones, when you continue to fight a battle against some force, you may withstand that force and perhaps stop its inroads from coming into your world. But this does not necessarily mean that you are able, by fighting this battle, to establish patterns of progress which are so essential for your future attainment of the power of purity.

"You can at one given moment invoke the power of purity by a simple word, saying: 'I am purity in action here. I am God's purity established forever, and the stream of light from the very heart of God that embodies all of his purity is flowing through me and establishing round about me the power of invincible cosmic purity which can never be requalified by the human.'"

Serapis thanks the Goddess of Purity for her instruction. "With your permission, I would like to take the words of your lecture and combine them with your prayer for purity so that the students may have them to repeat over and over to

*transmute that sense of impurity which may arise from time
to time."*

*She graciously consents and adds another short little
mantra for Purity that we can easily memorize and recite
throughout the day. Then she tells us that we may call to her
whenever we need her assistance for more purity in our lives.*

Prayer for Purity

In the name of my own beloved I AM Presence and Christ Self,
beloved Jesus the Christ and the Holy Spirit, I invoke the flame
of God's purity.

LORD, I AM worthy of thy purity. I would have thy
purity surge through me in a great cosmic burst to
remove from the screen of my mind, my thoughts and
my feelings every appearance of human vibratory action
and all that is impure in substance, thought or feeling.

Replace all that right now with the fullness of the
Mind of Christ and the Mind of God, the manifest
power of the Resurrection Spirit and the ascension
flame, that I may enter into the holy of holies of my
being and find the power of transmutation taking place
to free me forever from all discord that has ever manifested in my world.

I AM purity in action here, I AM God's purity established forever, and the stream of light from the very heart
of God that embodies all of his purity is flowing through
me and establishing round about me the power of invincible cosmic purity which can never be requalified by the
human.

Here I AM, take me, O God of purity. Assimilate me
and use me in the matrices of release for the mankind of
earth. Let me not only invoke purity for myself, but also
let me invoke purity for every part of life. Let me not
only invoke purity for my family, but also for all the

family of God neath the canopy of heaven.

I thank Thee and I accept this manifest right here and now with full power as the purity and authority of thy words spoken through me to produce the instantaneous manifestation of thy cosmic purity in my four lower bodies, intensifying hourly and accelerating those bodies until they attain the frequency of the ascension flame.

I AM Pure

By God's desire from on high,
Accepted now as I draw nigh,
Like falling snow with star-fire glow,
Thy blessed purity does bestow
Its gift of love to me.

I AM pure, pure, pure
By God's own word.
I AM pure, pure, pure,
O fiery sword.
I AM pure, pure, pure,
Truth is adored.

Descend and make me whole,
Blessed Eucharist, fill my soul.
I AM thy law, I AM thy light,
O mold me in thy form so bright!

Beloved I AM! Beloved I AM!
Beloved I AM![3]

A Reminder

Let us not forget this information, for the masters warn us that although we may believe and accept the Goddess of Purity's teaching that we are worthy, that we are a son or daughter of God, sometimes we may find ourselves affirming, "I am just no good. I am not worthy after all."

When you say, "I am no good," you are condemning the spark

of God, the I AM, within you. You are a spirit spark from God; you contain a portion of Almighty God within the secret chamber of your heart. And when you say, "I am not worthy," you are saying, "God in me is not worthy." And Saint Germain tells us that this is more dangerous than condemning our neighbors.

At this moment God Meru, a mighty being of great attainment, enters the room. He and his lovely twin flame, the Goddess Meru, are masters of the Temple of Illumination, an etheric focus at Mount Meru near Lake Titicaca in the Andes mountains in South America. At their retreat they maintain the focus of the feminine ray for the earth. The focus of the masculine ray is in the Himalayas. God Meru has given extensive teaching on self-condemnation and how to overcome it. Serapis Bey invites him to speak to us today.

Overcoming Self-Condemnation

God Meru begins his teaching:

"The majority of mankind in this very hour are burdened with a sense of condemnation which stifles creativity, stifles the beauty of the Godhead—the potential to bring forth the science of light, the music of the spheres, a golden-age culture.

"People walk the streets feeling unworthy of life itself. God in you is worthy to be adored! God in you is worthy to be joyous, to be upheld! If you are burdened with a sense of the consciousness of sin, then I say, what is your consciousness of God? What do you think of God if you make sin so real that you can never be released from the bondage of sin? Is God aware of all that? I tell you, nay. And if he is not aware of it, why should you give it even a flicker of your conscious attention?

"I say, O precious children of the sun, be not burdened with a sense of guilt, for there is no condemnation in God. But the demons and the fallen ones stand before you to condemn you night and day. And they whisper here and they whisper there and they tell you what a terrible person you are, what a miserable sinner you are, and that there is just no hope for your salvation.

"You stop all progress as long as you conceive of yourself as a sinner. Has the Creator lost his power to forgive, to transmute, to dissolve sin? Nay. Our God is a God of mercy and a consuming fire. Prove him, therefore, as he has commanded you to do. Prove his law.

"How do you do this? You simply say, 'In the name of Jesus the Christ, I cast all that is less than the Christ into the flame. O God, consume it. I ask it. Hear my plea and answer. I accept it done this hour in full power in fulfillment of the promise of the Creator.'

"Some of you sit in the seat of the scornful. You are scornful toward yourselves. You condemn yourselves because you think that you are not what you ought to be, that you have not made a great enough effort. Perhaps you forgot to pray this morning, or you did not have the time. Will you live in condemnation of yourself throughout the day? Or if you, through indiscretion, commit an act of sin for which you have sincere regret, will you be burdened by your own self-condemnation all the days of your life, thinking that you are unacceptable to God?

"Finally, the end result of self-condemnation is rebellion against the Deity, for man cannot live in self-condemnation; and thus he must throw off what he imagines to be the angry God who is condemning him. Therefore, he can only find his freedom by denying God totally. But who has created this God of condemnation but man himself, in his dissatisfaction with himself?"

Dealing with Self-Condemnation

As we take some time to meditate on our propensity for self-condemnation, we remember that we read in Habakkuk, "Thou art of purer eyes than to behold evil and canst not look on iniquity."[4] Then we realize that is why we have the Mediator, the Christ Self, who sees both the perfection of our I AM Presence and the problems that remain in our world. He does not condemn us, for he is aware that we are yet in the state of overcoming. Thus it is not God who condemns us, we condemn ourselves. It seems to be even more difficult for us to forgive ourselves than to forgive others!

When we say that we'll never condemn ourseves again, that's the best time for this vibration to come right back at us. We must be tested over and over again to be sure that we have finally eliminated self-condemnation from our world.

For it's not when the sky is blue and the birds are singing and the light of the masters is in your heart that your time of testing comes. It comes when you're tired, when you've been up most of the night with a sick baby, when you have a cold, when you have a problem at work that you can't seem to solve, when your checkbook won't balance or when your roommate is noisy as you are trying to write your term paper. This is the time when you need to hold fast and remember, "This is a test!"

That's when your self-condemnation may come back to you, yet all you need to do is say, "God Meru, help me. I'm sorry I went back into this vibration, but help me. Help me rise higher." Each time you remember to stop and call for help, you're going to be one step nearer the top of the pyramid of your ascension.

So just because you vowed today to stop self-condemnation, don't think that you will never fall back into it again. And if you reinforce the whole negative spiral, it will hold you down instead of lifting you up. Kuthumi once told us, "You can't stop a bird from lighting on your head, but you don't have to let him make a nest there."

These words of Kuthumi always make me chuckle. And although most of us don't have the attainment right now to completely stop the negative spiral of our thoughts, we don't have to keep reinforcing them. We can have simple mantras at our fingertips such as:

"O God, help me."
"I am a child of the light."
"God is my victory, victory, victory."
"Get thee behind me, Satan."[5]
"I can do all things through Christ which strengtheneth me."[6]

These are some of the resources we need at our fingertips that will immediately chase off that bird before he makes his nest.

Serapis thanks God Meru for his instruction, then turns to his class: "Dear hearts, I sense a vibration of anxiety in the room tonight. You have been concentrating so thoroughly on Master Meru's teachings and thinking perhaps that you are probably guilty of condemning yourself at times. Let's relax and enjoy the radiation of the violet flame as we repeat together Saint Germain's mantra: 'I AM a being of violet fire! I AM the purity God desires!'

"Now let's contemplate self-condemnation from another angle."

Effects of Self-Condemnation

So many of us are constantly tired. I've heard people say, "I can't do anything. I just came home from work and I'm absolutely exhausted." Well, in the first place, the master Saint Germain has said, "You have access to all the energy in the world if you will just call to me."

Our own individualized I AM Presence constantly showers down light from our Causal Body upon us. And Saint Germain says, "If you don't have that faith, call to me and I will give you my energy."

You may be tired simply because of self-condemnation. You may actually be practicing witchcraft and black magic against yourself. And Morya says, "Stop it! Stand up! Realize you are a son of God, a spark of God's immortal fire. You are meant to be immortal, not this piece of clay with which you are too prone to identify."

Many people are even suffering from diseases or impediments that are the direct result of their own condemnation of themselves. El Morya says, "O precious hearts, arise and be free, and Christ shall give thee light. You must be free of this sense of sin if you are to progress one foot forward on the Path. You stop all progress as long as you conceive of yourself as a sinner."

There is one more vital thing we must consider before we leave this subject of self-condemnation. Do you know that to forgive is to forget? If you are constantly revolving in your mind your supposed imperfections, how you fell short of the mark you set for yourself, you have not yet forgiven yourself because you have not yet forgotten.

Serapis speaks and says, "I would like to close with this thought: "So simple and childlike are the attributes of the kingdom that men overlook them and thus they pass them by. The blessings of God are all around life everywhere."

God Meru has given us a beautiful little mantra which you can use to affirm your worth as a son or daughter of God. You may want to personalize it as "I am a Child of the Light" and sing it to yourself over and over and over again until you really accept the fact that you are a child of the light.

You Are a Child of the Light

You are a child of the light
You were created in the Image Divine
You are a child of infinity
You dwell in the veils of time
You are a son of the Most High!

∾ *If you wish to further enhance your study before proceeding to Chapter 9, you will find exercises on p. 225.*

Chapter Nine

Violet Flame for Forgiveness

As Serapis Bey enters the classroom and surveys the students he says, "Ah, I see in your auras that you have struggled mightily this last week to eradicate self-condemnation from your worlds. But remember, beloved ones, Saint Germain teaches that 'it is the sense of struggle that makes the struggle.'"

The Violet Flame

There is a way out! And that way comes through the mercy of the violet flame. Instead of just beating at windmills, so to speak, sometimes it is necessary to withdraw from the problem and give invocations to the violet flame to see how quickly and easily resolution and forgiveness can come.

The violet flame is a "cosmic eraser." It offers us a way to shorten the days of karma so that we may quickly enter into the path to the ascension. It's even written in Mark, "For the elect's sake, whom he hath chosen, he hath shortened the days."[1]

Truly, the gift of the violet flame is God's mercy and grace for us in this age. It is the flame of forgiveness that we invoke through prayer and put into practice through service. Thus we can transmute our karma of centuries past and prepare our souls for the ascension. This violet all-consuming flame is the combination of the blue flame of power with the pink flame of love, which then becomes the universal solvent of mercy, transmutation and forgiveness.

The Master El Morya Speaks of the Violet Flame

Serapis says, "I have a surprise for you tonight. I have several times quoted from El Morya's teachings, but now I should like you to meet him in person. El Morya is Lord of the First Ray and Master of the Retreat of the Will of God in Darjeeling, India. He has written several books on the violet flame, an aspect of God's mercy that he believes is essential for each soul on the Path."

At this moment a master who is almost seven feet tall strides quickly into the room. He wears a long white robe and a sparkling turban. We can almost feel the blue flame crackle from him as he greets us.

"Good evening, students of the will of God. As you hear me speak or read my words, you can begin to experience the marvelous action of the violet flame coursing through your veins, penetrating the layers of the physical temple—the bloodstream, the nervous system, the brain—pressing through the chakras, swirling through the etheric body, passing over the pages of the written record of your incarnations on earth.

"Line by line, letter by letter, the flame—intelligent, luminous, directed by the mind of God—sets free the energies, electron by electron, of all past misuses of the sacred fire. And thus not one jot or tittle of the law of karma shall pass until all be fulfilled in the freedom of the violet fire.

"The violet flame comes forth from that aspect of the white light that is called the seventh ray. It is indeed the seventh-ray aspect of the Holy Spirit. Just as the sunlight passing through a prism is refracted into the rainbow of the seven color rays, so through the consciousness of the Holy Spirit the light of the Christ is refracted for mankind's use in the planes of Matter.

"Now let us examine what happens when the violet fire is applied to the recalcitrant conditions of the human consciousness. When, as an act of your free will, you make the call to the violet flame and you surrender these unwanted, untoward conditions into the flame, the fire instantaneously begins the work of breaking down the particles of substances.

"These are part of the mass accumulation of hundreds and even thousands of incarnations when in ignorance you

allowed to register—through your consciousness, through your attention, thoughts and feelings, words and actions—all of the degrading conditions to which the human race is heir." [2]
He ceases speaking and allows us to assimilate his words.

The Seventh-Ray Aspect of the Holy Spirit

As we meditate on these concepts, we see that when we invoke forgiveness, the violet flame bursts like violet, purple, pink fireworks in our aura and dissolves the unpleasant conditions in our world. Then as we continue to invoke it, it intensifies until great spheres of energy are going forth from our heart and inundating the world.

We may visualize a loved one, a child, a self-styled enemy, a political figure, an entire city, the government, the whole nation or the planet becoming the recipient of waves and waves of this wine of forgiveness.

You may be wondering, why have I never heard about the violet flame before? Because not all that was passed from Jesus Christ to his disciples has been recorded or preserved for our use. Many of the inner mysteries, including the knowledge of the violet flame, the I AM Presence and the science of invocation through the spoken Word, were taught privately by Jesus to his apostles, the holy women and those closest to him in his Galilean ministry.

Jesus did not give all his teachings to the multitudes who assembled to hear him preach. In addition, many of Jesus' teachings have been deleted from the Bible or their meaning tampered with by succeeding church councils.

John the Baptist spoke of this sacred fire when he said: "One mightier than I cometh, the latchet of whose shoes I am not worthy to unloose: he shall baptize you with the Holy Ghost and with fire." [3] This is what Jesus imparted in his teachings, in his forgiveness of sin. It was the conveyance of fire so that sins were forgiven and karma dissolved. Thereby the lame could walk, the deaf could hear, the blind could see.

An Invocation to the Violet Flame

El Morya has explained to us how to invoke the violet flame:

"If you would have the benefit of this miraculous energy, you have but to make the call. For the call compels the answer. But the call is a very special call. It is not the demand of the human consciousness but the command of your Real Self, or Christ Self, your own true being, the mediator between the I AM Presence and the soul. Thus you declare:

"In the name of the Christ Self and in the name of the living God, I call forth the energies of the sacred fire from the altar within my heart. In the name of the I AM THAT I AM, I invoke the violet flame to blaze forth from the center of the threefold flame, from the white-fire core of my own I AM Presence, multiplied by the momentum of the blessed Ascended Master Saint Germain. I call forth that light to penetrate my soul and to activate my soul memory of freedom and the original blueprint of my soul's destiny.

"I call forth the violet transmuting flame to pass through my four lower bodies and through my soul consciousness to transmute the cause and core of all that is less than my Christ-perfection, all that is not in keeping with the will of God for my lifestream. And I accept it done this hour in full power."[4]

El Morya Resumes His Teaching

El Morya continues to instruct us on the violet flame:

"When the violet flame is invoked, it loosens the dense substance and passes through and transforms that darkness into light. And each time a measure of energy is freed, a measure of a man ascends to the plane of God-awareness.

"As you begin to use the violet flame, you will experience feelings of joy, lightness, hope and newness of life as though clouds of depression were being dissolved by the very sun of your own being.

"Lord Zadkiel, Archangel of the Seventh Ray, made certain

that chelas of the new age would understand the joyousness of the flame, and so he called it the violet singing flame. Indeed, this flaming presence causes the very atoms and molecules of your being to 'sing' as they resume their normal frequency and are therefore brought into 'pitch' with the keynote of your own lifestream, your own I AM Presence.

"The violet flame forgives as it frees, consumes as it transmutes, clears the records of past karma (thus balancing your debts to life), equalizes the flow of energy between yourself and other lifestreams, and propels you into the arms of the living God.

"Day by day you are ascending higher and higher in the planes of consciousness of your Christ Self as you use the scrubbing action of the violet flame and feel how the very walls of your mental body are scoured.

"You can think of the action in your desire body as the dunking of your emotions in a chemical solution of purple liquid that dissolves the dirt that has accumulated for decades about the latticework of your feeling world.

"Every day and in every way the violet flame flushes out and renews your body cells, the cells of your mind and the globule of your soul, polishing the jewel of consciousness until it glistens in the sunlight."[5]

El Morya concludes his instruction with a courteous "Thank you" and a gracious bow and leaves the room quickly. But some of us think that we detect a twinkle in his eye as he passes us.

Serapis Bey rises and says, "I suspect that some of you may still be having difficulties visualizing the violet flame even after we have had instruction from Saint Germain and El Morya. Would any one like to come to the lectern and share with the class any method of visualization that works for you?"

A young woman walks to the front of the classroom and begins to address the class.

"The easiest way for me to visualize transmutation taking place is just to let my imagination run riot—seeing the violet flame interpenetrating every atom and cell of my body, my mind, my emotions and even the organs of my physical body.

"I happen to have had problems with my heart, and so I have been practicing seeing my heart surrounded and inter-penetrated by the mercy of the violet flame. And by the grace of God, I am feeling much better.

"The masters have given us the healing thought-form for our use. In my mind's eye, I envision flames of white, blue and green, forming an ovoid of light enfolding any organ with which I am having a problem. And then I am sure to surround the entire organ with plenty of beautiful, singing, crackling violet flame. I have an artist's rendition of the healing thought-form hanging on the wall in my bedroom to remind me to make calls to the violet flame for healing."

Serapis thanks the young woman and directs us to resume our study of the violet flame.

Violet Flame Seen in Meditation

All who have walked the path of the ascension have come into the awareness of the violet flame. Many saints, as they knelt before the altars of the great cathedrals of the world, have suddenly, in the heights of their meditation and communion with God, been transported and seen blazing upon the altar this beautiful, roaring, pulsating, singing violet flame. The same experience has happened to many yogis and holy men in their caves in the Himalayas, to nuns and monks in their cells and to devotees of all faiths and cultures throughout the world.

This has been a private revelation to them from the depths of their devotion. And through this revelation they have earned their ascension and have not remained to teach this knowledge to the world. Many devotees, unbeknownst to themselves, succeed in invoking the violet flame through the power of intercessory prayer. They call forth those activities of the sacred fire of

God, which in the West are usually termed the action of the Holy Spirit and in the East are related to the destruction of all that is unreal by Lord Shiva.

At the end of this instruction, one student hesitantly raises her hand. "Beloved Serapis, would I be intruding if I related an incident which I experienced that relates directly to this teaching?"

Serapis nods his approval and she begins.

"I would like to recount an incident which occurred to a woman before she had heard of the violet flame. The young woman said that she had traveled to Asia and Malaysia to research patterns which she could use in her fabric designs. In addition to her research she planned to visit monasteries and have a spiritual retreat.

"One day in deep meditation in a Buddhist monastery, she actually saw the violet flame pulsating on the altar. This event so touched her life that she spent the next several years traveling around, asking the monks and everyone she met if they had ever heard of the violet flame. She described her meditation to them, but no one could give her any answers.

"Finally, as she was ready to fly home from Singapore, she saw one of our posters advertising a lecture on the violet flame by students of Elizabeth Clare Prophet and giving the dates of the next session of Summit University in Santa Barbara. She joined our group as soon as she returned home."

Serapis thanks the student and continues his instruction on the violet flame.

"The next subject I would like us to consider this evening," Serapis says, "is forgiveness—a concept closely allied to the violet flame that we have been discussing."

Forgiveness

It can take us lifetimes of meditation to arrive at the place where we can see the violet flame, yet Saint Germain so loved the world that he was trusted to bring this instruction to us so that we could have it in printed form.

However, this dispensation was costly to him. He offered the Lords of Karma the momentum of the violet flame garnered within his heart chakra and within his Causal Body as a gift of light and energy for mankind that they might experiment with the alchemy of self-transformation through the sacred fire.

Saint Germain tells us that the process of the ascension is one of complete forgiveness. To this end he has offered us the violet flame of transmutation, given to us in mercy from God and the Karmic Board.

The initiation of forgiveness is one of the most difficult on the Path. It sounds so simple yet is so hard, because it is necessary to forgive ourselves as well as to forgive others. Forgiving ourselves is the hard part.

We have already seen how self-condemnation hinders our ability to forgive ourselves. And Kuan Yin, the Goddess of Mercy, says, "In forgiveness there comes renewable opportunity to fulfill the law. And without forgiveness, little progress can be made." Therefore, to reenter the walk with God, we need forgiveness.

We need to be able to confess to God and tell him what we have done that is not in keeping with his law. Until we tell him about it and ask for his forgiveness, we keep a sense of guilt, fear and shame and above all a sense of separation from him. Today this can be seen to manifest in all kinds of mental and emotional illnesses, split personalities, hatred of father and mother, hatred of children and many other problems to which modern society has fallen prey. The path back to the guru, the inner Christ, is found through forgiveness.

Forgiveness is not something we need to invoke only for ourselves. We need to invoke it for every part of life—all who have ever wronged us, all whom we have ever wronged.

Saint Germain teaches us that when we invoke forgiveness we must have intense love in our heart. We need to let others know that we forgive them and that we want them to forgive us.

And we need to humbly say, "I've done wrong, and I ask you and God to forgive me."

Sometimes we can become depressed, unhappy and even resentful because of some event or person in our lives that we just cannot forgive and forget. When this occurs, if we could only realize that perhaps this depression or resentment is the result of karma coming back for redemption, we would sweep the violet flame through those records and get on with our lives.

You know, we have been told that sometimes we may be paying the penalty for something we did to that person in a prior life. Of course, we don't remember our past and thus we feel that we are the one who has been wronged. But Portia, Saint Germain's twin flame, has said, "There is no injustice anywhere in the universe."

Unfortunately, we can't remember the event that caused what today we see as an injustice. But assuming that it was not an injustice, we should now get serious with our violet flame decrees until we are able to forgive whatever or whoever has been troubling us.

Methods of Transmutation

When we invoke the flame of forgiveness, let us realize that our own Christ Self can be our psychiatrist, our psychologist, our minister, our priest, our rabbi, our friend—the one to whom we should go daily to unburden ourselves.

Mark Prophet used to say that the American Indians would make a circle around the campfire at night to discuss the events of the day. All that had happened that they didn't like, they would throw into the flames. The same principle is taught in every religion in the world. If we would put our troubles into the flame at night, we could then rest in peace.

Much insomnia is the result of not releasing our daily karma, our daily burdens, and therefore we are not at peace with ourselves and with God. To realize true peace within, each of us must find our own way of unburdening ourselves.

Here is another thoughtform that you may use in addition to the American Indian's circle around the fire. Pack up all your troubles. Visualize everything that's bothering you. Put it in an old knapsack. Tie it up by the corners. Swing it over your back. Walk out on a pier and dump it in the ocean.

Worrying about it now won't do you a bit of good. You've already thrown in your worries, and so you can't possibly take them back and worry about them again tomorrow because they have sunk to the bottom of the ocean.

You now have a whole new day ahead of you—a whole new opportunity! So do whatever it takes to cleanse your mind before you go to sleep. Surrender your burdens to God and then don't pick them up again in the morning.

El Morya has given us a mantra for invoking forgiveness that is a powerful aid to transmutation:

> I AM forgiveness acting here,
> Casting out all doubt and fear,
> Setting men forever free
> With wings of cosmic victory.
>
> I AM calling in full power
> For forgiveness every hour.
> To all life in every place
> I flood forth forgiving grace.

Karmic Board Letters

If you are still suffering from guilt and can't quite rid yourself of it, there is one more method I might suggest. Write a letter to the Karmic Board. As we learned in chapter two, the Karmic Board is comprised of eight ascended masters, each representing one of the seven rays and the eighth ray of integration. The Lords of Karma dispense justice to this system of worlds, adjudicating karma, mercy and judgment on behalf of every lifestream.

To help free yourself from guilt or remorse, you might

actually write a confession letter and address it to God or to the Karmic Board. Write it in ink with your own handwriting; don't type it. You might begin with "I am sincerely sorry for my transgressions and I'm casting them upon the mercy of the violet flame." And then list them in your letter.

Be sure to include your hopes, your plans and even your burdens in your letter, not just your confessions. Write a letter to God and pour out your heart to him, asking him to adjust your plans according to his will. Then burn your letter safely in your fireplace or in a metal pan and accept God's forgiveness. As the angels bear the smoke to the Lords of Karma, your petition is acted upon.

This can be a great release for people who have been suffering under a sense of guilt. Get in the habit of writing often to the ascended masters. Learn to feel comfortable talking to them.

The Mercy of the Law

And now, Serapis says, "Please welcome again the Ascended Lady Master Kuan Yin, our Goddess of Mercy. You may remember, she addressed you briefly as we were discussing the violet flame."

Kuan Yin smiles at the class as she begins her teaching on mercy.

"The mercy of the law is like a two-way street. It is the signal which you send to God and the signal which he returns. The thoughtform of a two-way street means a give-and-take with God. If you expect mercy from God, then you must give mercy to every part of life. The fulfillment of the law of mercy must be for the ultimate liberation of each and every soul. Thus, as we forgive life, life forgives us.

"The action of mercy and forgiveness is the setting aside of karma for a time to give one the opportunity to find God, to find the Holy Spirit and to accept Christ as one's saviour. But when one has found Christ and is centered in the flame, then the mercy of the law considers it the full circle of that

mercy to deliver to the individual that karma which was set aside, the weight of that sin which must now be balanced."

Kuan Yin paused here, giving us a little time for further thought.

Forgive and Forget

The law of forgiveness is also known as the law of containment whereby our misdeeds and debts to life are set aside temporarily until the soul has received enough knowledge of the law and has become strong enough to pay the penalty in full for her past errors.

Often people feel a sense of injustice when problems keep occurring in their lives while their neighbors seem to be able to go through life unscathed. The answer to this seeming inequality is that when one sets one's foot firmly on the path of the ascension, the soul asks for the opportunity to quickly balance her last remaining karmic debts. The neighbor who seems to lead such a charmed life may not yet have embarked upon the path of initiation and is experiencing a much slower return of karma.

As the saying goes: "You get what you pay for," and the price for the ascension is high.

Time and time again we have all heard the saying "Let bygones be bygones. Forgive and forget!" Kuan Yin has often told us that to really forgive, we must completely clear the record of the event. She said that if we could resurrect the memory of a wrong that was done to us long ago, we had not truly forgiven the person for it.

She said that instead of forgiving, "You have hardened your heart. You have stored a record as a squirrel with his nuts. Deep within the subconscious, deep in the etheric plane, you have stored the record of that wrong. You have not released it into the flame. You have not been willing to let go and let God be free to express through those who have wronged you, and those whom you have wronged."

So we can see how training in the law of forgiveness is

necessary, for there is a difference between the forgiveness of sins and their transmutation. For example, someone may steal your purse and later tell you that he is sorry he took it. You may forgive him, but the matter is not closed, karmically-speaking, until he returns the purse to you with every penny intact or makes whatever restitution is possible.

Forgiveness is not the balancing of karma; it is the setting aside of karma whereby you are given the freedom to make things right without that heavy burden of sin.

If you have sincerely tried and still cannot forgive someone or something that has happened to you, you may need a few sessions with a professional therapist. There may be some scars remaining from past lives about which you are completely unaware. Inner child work may unlock these blocks that are keeping you from your mastery.

Miracles have happened in people's lives from just a few appointments with a qualified psychologist. Don't hesitate to accept this method of healing if you cannot resolve situations in your life that are bothering you. A word of caution, however. The ascended masters do not approve of hypnotism because by this means you are leaving your consciousness open to someone else's control.

Kuan Yin returns to ask us if we can be as little children and pretend that it is Christmas today. She says, "Will you do something for me as I bring you the tide of mercy?

"Will you write your Christmas list as you would a letter to Santa—but write it to me and list all whom you can remember that you have failed to forgive or who have failed to forgive you—and give me that Christmas list? Give me also your heart flame with the authority to inundate life, specifically those whom you name, with an increment of mercy from my temple (located in the etheric octave over Peking) and from my altar.

"Then, to start your New Year, forgive yourself all wrongs, all infractions of the Great Law. Will you truly for-

give, which is to forget and to forsake the past?" Then Kuan Yin sums up her entire teaching on mercy and forgiveness as she says very simply, "our hearts need to melt, for we need to forgive in order to be forgiven."

As we all nod our heads in agreement, we remember that Serapis Bey stated the same principle before in a slightly different way. He said, "In order to ascend, you must abandon your past to God."

∹ *If you wish to further enhance your study before proceeding to Chapter 10, you will find exercises on p. 226.*

CHAPTER TEN

‖

Karma

Serapis Bey asks for a show of hands from those who still have unanswered questions or would like to make a comment. Immediately two hands shoot up at the same time. One young man says that he is still interested in an explanation of karma and a woman over on the far right says that she would like that also. Serapis replies that he has chosen karma as our topic for tonight's lesson, for although he has referred to karma from time to time, he feels that now is the time to explore the subject in depth.

How We Made Karma

Each of us is a spirit spark of God who came down into embodiment to help the world. We volunteered to come, especially those of us who were once angels, saying, "Oh, if I only had a body, I could help these people of earth."

Well, we received our bodies all right, but instead of being as much help as we wanted to be, we became enmeshed in the troubles of the people of earth, in world karma. We've been here long enough and now it's time for us to balance the last vestiges of that karma and ascend back to the heart of God.

We must understand that there is both good and bad karma—karma can be both negative and positive. We usually associate the word *karma* with negativity, but all our good works from all our many embodiments are stored in our Causal Body.

Little progress is made in other planes toward balancing karma, for it is here in the physical world that we made our karma and here that we must balance it. And therefore, let none think that they will live forever in these four lower bodies. They are but vehicles of consciousness that are loaned to us by God, as all God's energy is on loan to us, so that we might prove our mastery of free will.

The Bible passage that describes it best is Galatians 6:7, "Whatsoever a man soweth, that shall he also reap." None can defeat this law. For as Serapis has told us, "Men cannot build immortal bodies out of mortal substance; they cannot build out of mortal thought immortal ideas, nor build out of mortal feelings divine feelings that enfold the world and create the Great Pyramid of Life."[1]

Procrastination

El Morya has warned that "procrastination is a disease that is the death of the chela." And Serapis himself has said: "There is a tendency among men that is encouraged by the brothers of shadow and the sons of Belial, who masquerade at times as angels of light, to postpone the salvation of the soul to some distant tomorrow or to the life hereafter.

"The ascension must be desired, not as a mechanism of escape from responsibilities or worldly duties. It must be desired as the culmination of a lifetime of service in the will of God."[2]

But the masters have cautioned that the end can never justify the means. They do not agree with the tenet "Let us do evil that good may come."[3] The means—the way we do something—is every bit as important as the outcome in the eyes of the Brotherhood.

Karma Is Never Punishment

Our karma is not meant to tear us apart; it is supposed to teach us where we went wrong so that we will not repeat our error.

The Goddess of Purity once said, "The law of karma, blessed ones, is not intended to act as a lash, to tear apart the souls of men. The law of karma is intended to instruct and to cause mankind to approach the throne of grace without fear, with the clearness of mind and being that will render them able to receive the pure vibratory action of Almighty God."

Karma is never for punishment, but because it hurts, we

experience it many times as a sense of punishment. Yet God, in his great forgiveness and love, rather than condemning us to everlasting punishment for our mistakes, allows us to be on the receiving end of our deeds so that we can learn from them and never repeat them.

Therefore, let us pray urgently that we understand that all things come to us for our education, whether as returning karma or as the seeming injustices of life.

There Is No Injustice

Portia, the Goddess of Justice and Opportunity, says emphatically, "There is no injustice anywhere in the universe!" Judgment is totally an action of the law. What may seem to be unfair to us today may only be our just retribution for having done the exact same thing to someone else in a former life. Of course, we do not remember the incident that is playing out before our eyes today.

Nevertheless, because we went out of the way in our sojourn on earth, God has the right to test us to earn our return to his heart. Elizabeth Clare Prophet gave a lecture in which she said, "God has the right to test the mettle of one who would be with him in heaven. And therefore, you may have a burden upon you in this hour that is not caused by karma at all, but is an opportunity for you to gain mastery and witness to the glory of God and the use of his mighty name, I AM THAT I AM. For this mighty name itself contains the power to heal, and God wants you to know that."

So, if we can accept what is happening to us as justice, whether it be justice by testing, by temptation or by karma, then we will submit to the law and say, "O God, help me with this problem. Help me with this condition. I accept thy judgments. I know that I must deal with this situation for my mastery. Please show me how."

And we are buoyed up in our hearts, even in the most extreme situation by saying, "There is no injustice anywhere in the universe!"

The Patience of Job

Before we leave the subject of testing, let's look at the Book of Job in the Old Testament. Job was an upright, good servant of God whom Satan wanted to test. He wanted Job to curse the name of God as a result of the tribulation that would come upon him. God allowed this test but stipulated that Satan might not kill Job.

And we know how the story went. All sorts of terrible things came upon Job and yet he still refused to curse God. In the end, everything that he had lost was restored to him many times over. Perhaps we need to truly have the patience of Job when our troubles seem about to overwhelm us.

Paul also suffered greatly when he was cast into prison by the Romans. Yet while he was in prison he used the opportunity to commune with God and to write letters to his flock, and he was delivered from prison by an angel. Some of the greatest books of the New Testament are our legacy from Paul's imprisonment. Not only Paul, but many of the great martyrs and heroes of history have been imprisoned.

It is not whether or not we are behind bars that counts. It is whether we are the prisoner of our own ego, lust, envy, resentment, hatred or self-condemnation. What interests the masters is how we react to situations. The Buddha Maitreya often uses the events of everyday life as initiations to test us. Once again we must remember Portia's teaching that "there is no injustice anywhere in the universe."

Preparation for Tests

According to God's law, we cannot be given a test for which we have not been prepared. The difficult part, however, is that we have been prepared in the inner retreats and often do not consciously remember this preparation when the test comes. We need to learn to know the law and study the teachings of the ascended masters. We also need to put on the Christ consciousness and know right from wrong, for failure to do so can cause us to fail a test in the hour of initiation. Serapis says, "To be ignorant is understandable, but to know not that one is ignorant is a tragedy of considerable dimension." And in the Bible we read, "Get wisdom: and with all thy getting, get understanding."[4]

Love God

The answer to our problems is to love God so much that we do not need to satisfy every human desire. We don't always have to appease the carnal mind and give it what it wants so that we will have a moment's peace. Nor do we have to engage our energies in imperfection.

Lord Lanto warns us, "I am well aware of the fact that all these matters appear simple on the surface. Often individuals who read our instruction are so struck by its simplicity that they cry out, 'But I already know that!'" But then he adds: "It is not what you know that counts, but what you do!"[5]

The Daily Descent of Karma

Elizabeth Clare Prophet teaches that the best way she can explain the descent of karma is that each day our karma comes down to us in a little brown paper bag. If we can rise early and give our prayers and fiats quickly before we go to work—or whatever is on our schedule—we can get a great percentage of that day's karma out of the way.

However, a portion of the day's karma that is sent our way may be from actions dating all the way back to our lives on Lemuria and Atlantis. If we don't clear it, it just sits on us all day long and piles up in our electronic belt.

Without being too concerned about it, we can accept that each day we are going to have a certain amount of karma returned to us because we asked for it and set ourselves on the path to the ascension. Our karma is also returning to us more speedily than to those not on the Path, but by the grace of God and by the mercy of the violet flame we can daily transmute it if we will.

Freedom from the bondage of karma can come only when the law of cause and effect has been fully worked out. Jesus himself revealed this law when he said, "Heaven and earth shall pass away but my words shall not pass away,"[6] and "One jot or one tittle shall in no wise pass from the law till all be fulfilled."[7]

By divine mercy and grace, individuals have had hidden from their eyes the extent to which they have lowered their standards throughout their lifetimes. Mercifully, we have had a veil of forgetfulness placed over our eyes at birth. Thus, we do not remember the things we have done in past lives when we didn't know the law and didn't realize what we were doing.

Think That Your Karma Is Light

It is better to think that one's karma is light rather than heavy. For when people think they have a heavy karma, they become worried or depressed about it and become lethargic, almost unwilling to begin paying off the karmic debt, feeling that it is too overpowering to contemplate.

If we feel we have a heavy karma, we may say, "What is the use? I just can't do it. I have so much going against me that there is no use even trying."

When individuals believe their karma to be light and they begin to release it swiftly into the sacred fire, a great feeling of joy sweeps through their being. Joy has the ability to cause us to relax and it can free us from problems that we may have carried for centuries.

Some people may shrug and say, "Well, it's just my karma" and stop trying. They just accept karma as extra weight without realizing that God offers us his mercy and grace to help us surmount it. Unfortunately, the karma is there—it's a fact. We cannot ignore it, for we created it in the first place.

However, there is another side to this equation: We can't just slide along day by day either, making little effort to balance our karma because we think everything will turn out all right in the end. Remember, we have been told that the ascension is not an automatic process. We have to work for it!

We have been given the knowledge of the violet flame to transmute our karma—all the misqualified energy in our electronic belt. And this comes not by our merit but by grace, by the love of God. It is his gift to us!

We have a choice. When we realize we have sent forth injustice and by cosmic justice that injustice will return to us, will we endure this karma forever? Will we multiply it again and create a bigger injustice because we are resentful? Or will we call upon the LORD, invoke his Holy Spirit, his violet flame, and ask that all life that we have ever wronged anywhere, anytime, be blessed and freed from this burden?

Grace

In our discussion of karma we must include the concept of grace. There is a way out and grace is a great part of it! I am sure that none of us could ever make it by ourselves. We try and try as hard as we can, and then the grace of God takes over and carries us the rest of the way home.

A song that you may have sung in Sunday school is called "Amazing Grace." One of the verses says, "'Tis grace hath brought me safe thus far and grace will lead me home." When you look back over all the millions of years of embodiments, see how wise it is to hold on to that concept of grace, for it can sustain you through many a dark day. Nevertheless, we have been offered our freedom at last and by his grace we will make it.

The Goddess of Purity Encourages Us On

At this point the Goddess of Purity enters the room and asks Serapis for permission to speak to the students for a moment. She is wearing a beautiful dress of a shimmering, crystalline substance—white and lined with a fabric of soft shell pink.

"Dear ones of the Light, I would like to encourage you by telling you that you have a saying here upon this planet that

'Rome was not built in a day.' Yet so many of you seem to feel when dealing with spiritual matters that if you do not over-come all of your afflictions and faults in one given moment, you are simply not living.

"Precious ones, let me give you the comfort of knowing that we who are in these higher octaves of light required a ter-rific amount of time in order to obtain our release from all of the pressures of life that surrounded us.

"Do you see, then, that if we ourselves required such an amount of time in order to obtain our own freedom and purity, if we are able to understand and look upon you with compassion, that God himself looks upon you with the com-passion of an infinite Father? He awaits the release in your being of purity's acceptance that will not fear to accept purity for yourself, that will not fear to accept purity now."

The room remained totally still as the Goddess of Purity ceased speaking. We had already been told that the ascended masters made their ascension in times that were often more dif-ficult than the present. Yet we could scarcely imagine as great a being as the Goddess of Purity needing time for her victory. It should certainly put our own everyday troubles in perspective!

The Goddess of Purity gracefully takes her leave of our classroom and our instruction continues. One of the students has a question on ill health. "Is being ill connected to karma in any way?" he asks. Serapis tells us that health can be related to karma, as well as to other factors.

Health Related to Karma

Ill health is prevalent in individuals for many reasons; part of it is psychosomatic. Part of it is caused by self-condemnation and part is caused by lack of protection. We need to be vigilant about our calls to Archangel Michael but much of ill health is related to, and in part caused by, untransmuted karma. Health, both good and bad, may be the result of past and present uses of energy.

Kuthumi says, "Good health encourages the steadfast flow

of energy. The reverse is also true. We cannot deny that there are good and bad energies, but let us remember that energy itself is really neither good nor bad. It is the qualification that is made of energy that determines its inherent manifestation."

All Energy is God. Energy can neither be created nor destroyed because it is of God. We have taken his pure energy and misqualified it— qualified it by our free will.

Again Kuthumi, our divine psychologist, gave this explanation when he said, "If you will consider the facts, (1) that God is boundless energy, (2) that man has been given a limited quantity of God's energy, and (3) that the energy which he has been given does comprise the content of the soul, you will be on the right track in your investigations of the self."[8]

The Crystal Cord

We once had access to much more light than we have today. Our crystal cord, our connection to God's energy, is now very narrow. We used to be bathed in a giant tube of light as was Methuselah in the Old Testament. He lived for nine hundred years, as did many others in that time, because their crystal cords were much larger.

Mankind misqualified energy on Lemuria and Atlantis through experiments and abuse of the sacred fire. Energy was misqualified through the commingling of animal and human life and many other activities not approved of by God.

In his mercy, God then limited the amount of light that we receive each day so that we would have less to misqualify. Thus with less energy, we could do less harm and the harm we did would not rebound upon us so fast.

World Karma

Another aspect of karma that we have not yet discussed is world karma. Serapis has spoken before about this, pointing out that some must rise to the challenge of bearing world karma. He says:

"The little child maturing to become the master cannot take

upon himself that cross of world karma because he is too busy carrying his own cross of selfishness and self-indulgence. As a result, many are not equipped to enter into the age of responsibility as the sons and daughters of God. Few are able to bear the sins of the world as Christ did when he hung upon the cross—the cross not of his own human karma, but the cross of the karma of the race.

"In every age there must be souls who are willing to bear a certain portion of world karma. In these times it is elemental life, the nature spirits, who bear that weight. Those among mankind who care at all to carry a little extra baggage are few and far between.

"Let the cross [of world karma] be transmuted daily. Let your cross be a cross of light so that even while you are balancing your karma you may carry the weight of world karma in this dark cycle. Let your burden be light. Let the cross of your karma become a cross of intense devotion and love. And let your burden be light, moment by moment, as you sense the victory of love.

"Therefore the bearing of the weight of world karma need not be a via dolorosa but a way of joy, a way of victory and overcoming. For as soon as that energy of world karma is given to you, you consecrate it to the Holy Spirit and the sacred fire. It is transmuted and, lo, your burden is light."[9]

Our Responsibility

Jesus bore our sins upon the cross for a certain period of time in the Piscean age, but that is only part of the story. He bore for us the world karma that was due at the beginning of the Piscean age until we could be strong enough to take it back and balance it ourselves. Now the responsibility is ours!

Service to Balance Karma

The more we know of the law, the more responsible we are for service to our fellowman. We have been told that one of the fastest ways to balance personal karma is through service to others. In fact, the masters have told us that "the reward for service is more service."

Many seem to feel they have no time for service in addition to their daily eight hours at work, yet you can always make time in your life for what you really want to do. Saint Germain says, "You can do anything if you love enough." And remember, he has also promised to give us his energy when we feel tired.

Meru tells us that service is our escape from the rounds of embodiments. So, "The key to freedom," he says, "is to serve and to search."

When we enter into the service of the LORD, we know that we are becoming whole through the process of regeneration. We give all that we are in service and when we empty ourselves each day, God fills us again with light. Each infilling is a rejuvenation, a regeneration. We are recharged so that we can give of ourselves again and again and again. And the more we are self-emptied, the more we are filled.

Serapis concludes by saying: "As you review this material, be sure that you do not fall into the trap of feeling that your karma is so heavy that there is no hope for you. Just because you have been introduced to the fact that you may now be balancing karma that you made on Lemuria and Atlantis, remember that you cannot see how much good karma is stored in the rings of your Causal Body. And to anyone with inner vision, your higher bodies are beautiful to behold. God bless you all, and rest well."

～*If you wish to further enhance your study before proceeding to Chapter 11, you will find exercises on p. 228.*

CHAPTER ELEVEN

❦

The Chart of Your Divine Self

As we enter our classroom in the retreat tonight, we see in the front of the room a beautiful translucent reproduction entitled, "The Chart of Your Divine Self." Serapis tells us that this is the true rendition of how we really look. We are not just physical men and women standing on the earth, for our Christ Self hovers above us in the atmosphere, and then above that is our God Presence—all tied to us by our crystal cord.

Serapis assures us that he will explain, as the evening progresses, how the trinity of the Father-Mother God, the Son or Mediator and the Holy Spirit are depicted in the Chart of Your Divine Self. (See color plate facing page 97.)

The Upper Figure

The upper figure is the I AM Presence, the I AM THAT I AM, the individualized presence of God in each of his sons and daughters.

The Causal Body, shown as seven color bands, surrounds the I AM Presence and contains the record of man's good works— all of God's energy that he has qualified positively in this life and in all his past lives. These records are stored here as his "treasure in heaven."

The Middle Figure

The middle figure in the Chart is the Mediator between God and man, our Christ Self, or Real Self. It has often been referred to as the Higher Mental Body, or Christ consciousness. It is the Christ of Jesus and the Christ of you and me.

Christianity has taught that only Jesus is the Christ. Through a mistaken explanation of Jesus as the only begotten Son of God

CHART OF YOUR DIVINE SELF

the Father, it teaches exclusive Sonship for Jesus and denies the God-potential and Christ-potential of all other souls.

The ascended masters teach that it is the destiny of all light-bearers to become the Son. The only begotten Son is one Christ and one saviour, the Universal Christ. And yet this Son is personified for each child of God in the person of our Christ Self. Everyone who becomes one with his Christ Self can be called the Christ and thus it is the destiny of each lightbearer to become the Son of God.

The Eucharist

In the ritual of Holy Communion Jesus opened the way for his disciples to reconnect with their Christ Self. He took one loaf, symbolizing the Universal Christ, broke it and said, "This is my body which is broken for you."[1] The body of the one Christ was then individualized for each one of us as the Christ Self.

Each piece of bread that Jesus gave to his disciples from the one loaf was the gift of himself. It was the gift of his Christhood. Each piece was a portion of his Universal Light Body and yet it was also the whole that is fragmented over and over again for every incoming soul. Therefore the potential to be the Christ is with us at the moment of our birth. Each time we return in a new body we again have the opportunity to know the Self as God, the I AM THAT I AM, and to know the Self as Christ.

Mark Prophet often told us that each one of us is a drop of water from the ocean. We have all the qualities of the ocean within that one drop and our destiny is to merge with God, our Real Self, as the drop becomes one with the ocean.

The difference between Jesus and the rest of us is that he had the full attainment of the Godhead dwelling in him. Inasmuch as we have not yet perfected our Christhood, we have our I AM Presence and Christ Self just above us to help us along the way. Our Christ Self (the middle figure in the Chart) overshadows us wherever we are and wherever we go.

Jesus, the Example

Jesus came to demonstrate the path of personal Christhood so that the children of the light could follow in his footsteps throughout the Piscean age and beyond. He is our example who showed us how to walk back home to the Father. The threefold flame and Christ Self are the means whereby every living soul who came forth from God may return to him through the grace of Jesus Christ.

Your own Christ Self, standing as the Mediator between God and you, is able to teach you and forgive your mistakes as you walk the path of overcoming. The Mediator bridges the gap between you and your I AM Presence and awakens your soul to her lost identity.

The Lower Figure

The lower figure in the Chart is shown enveloped in the violet flame within the tube of light. This tube of light descends from your I AM Presence in answer to your call and protects you twenty-four hours a day, as long as you remain harmonious. You can visualize this cylinder of brilliant white light around you beginning at your I AM Presence and extending to about thirty-six inches beneath your feet.

We are asked to give the violet flame and tube of light decree first thing in the morning when we get up and to repeat it throughout the day whenever we feel negative energies riding in upon us.

> Beloved I AM Presence bright,
> Round me seal your tube of light
> From ascended master flame
> Called forth now in God's own name.
> Let it keep my temple free
> From all discord sent to me.
>
> I AM calling forth violet fire
> To blaze and transmute all desire,

Keeping on in freedom's name
Till I AM one with the violet flame.

The Mediator, who is the Inner Teacher, overshadows this lower self, the soul evolving through the four planes of matter. The soul uses the vehicles of the four lower bodies (the etheric body, the mental body, the emotional body and the physical body) to balance karma and fulfill her divine plan.

As a disciple on the Path, you correspond to the lower figure. Your soul is the nonpermanent aspect of being which is made permanent through the ritual of the ascension. The first step you can take in reuniting with your I AM Presence is to develop a relationship with your Christ Self, who is your teacher, guardian and dearest friend. He is the voice of conscience speaking within your heart, showing you what is right and wrong.

The Crystal Cord

The crystal cord (referred to as the silver cord in Ecclesiastes[2]) is the stream of life that descends from the heart of the I AM Presence through the Christ Self to nourish and sustain the soul's four lower bodies. You can visualize the I AM Presence as floating somewhere between seven and seventy feet above your head, depending upon your state of consciousness and attunement.

Over this "umbilical cord" flows the energy of the Presence, entering the being of man at the crown and springing up as the divine spark, or threefold flame in the heart. It gives the impetus for the physical heartbeat as well as the pulsation of the threefold flame.

The Dove of the Holy Spirit

The dove of the Holy Spirit is shown just above the head of the Christ Self, descending from the Father. When the son of man puts on and becomes the Christ consciousness as Jesus did, he merges with his Christ Self. The Holy Spirit is upon him and the words of the Father, the beloved I AM Presence, are spoken,

"This is my beloved Son in whom I am well pleased; hear ye him."[3]

When this lifetime is finished, the I AM Presence withdraws the crystal cord, and the threefold flame returns to the level of the Christ. The soul, clothed in the etheric garment, rises to the highest level of her attainment to be taught by the ascended masters in their etheric retreats and prepared for her ascension or for her next embodiment.

Thus the Chart is a diagram—past, present and future—of your soul's pilgrimage to the Great Central Sun as year upon year you ascend the spiral staircase of life, drawing nigh to God as he draws nigh to you.

At the conclusion of the teaching, Serapis Bey remains on the platform. "I sense that there is someone who has something she would like to share with us, but she is a bit hesitant. Please come to the front of the room."

A young woman rises and shyly makes her way to the platform. She says, "I would like to testify to the power of the tube of light decree.

"I once had an experience where I actually heard the tube of light sing to me. My husband and I had closed our photography studio and were planning to come on staff with Mark and Elizabeth Prophet at The Summit Lighthouse in Santa Barbara.

"My elderly father-in-law had agreed to buy our home from us for cash. This sum would pay all our debts and allow us to go forth on our new life. One day, just two weeks before we were to leave, he arrived at our front door and said, 'This is nonsense. I am too old to buy a house.'

"My entire world crumbled in ruins at that moment— all our plans were a shambles.

"I got in my car to go to the bank to see about a loan, although I knew we would not receive the full amount we had planned on and would probably have to obtain a second mortgage. I knew that I should decree, but I was so com-

pletely shattered that I couldn't remember a single decree. After several minutes of panic, I suddenly heard the tube of light decree singing in my mind. I had never heard that there could be music to decrees. This descent of grace calmed me enough so that I could again make plans.

"When I returned home, there was a phone call from my father-in-law awaiting me. He said, 'Come over right away before I change my mind again. Drive me to the bank and I'll give you the cash right now.' Believe me, I didn't waste any time. I don't think we realize how tenderly God cares for us if we will only trust him completely."

As we file out of our class tonight, there are smiles on all our faces. Perhaps we are hearing the song of the tube of light in our hearts!

᠁*If you wish to further enhance your study before proceeding to Chapter 12, you will find exercises on p. 228.*

CHAPTER TWELVE

The Science of the Spoken Word

Serapis begins his lecture by saying that the teaching most vital to self-mastery is the science of invocation. This includes the art of decreeing, or spoken prayer. The goal of effective decrees is to unlock the energies of your Real Self. You will never know until you try just how much of God's light you can actually draw down into your world through these decrees.

The Importance of Spoken Prayer

The Book of John opens with the words: "In the beginning was the Word, and the Word was with God, and the Word was God." The use of the spoken Word, or spoken prayer, is at the heart of all true religions. Christians, Jews, Moslems, Hindus, Buddhists and others offer their devotions to God in the form of prayer, mantra and decrees.

The science of spoken prayer has been practiced for many centuries by adepts in the Far East and by Western mystics. The ascended masters instruct their disciples today in the lost art of invocation that was practiced on Atlantis and Lemuria and even before that in earlier golden ages.

"Let there be light!"[1] was the first decree ever spoken by the Father. The response was instantaneous and the world was born by the power of the spoken Word.

In Isaiah we read, "Concerning the works of my hands, command ye me."[2] Here God is asking us not only to petition him for grace and mercy but also to command him—to command his energy to do his will in and through us, to work his works upon earth and in our lives. He is, in fact, telling us that we must command him to descend into our beings if we would experience him in consciousness. Why is that?

God gave us the gift of free will and the responsibility to take dominion over the earth, and thereby he relinquished his command of the earth to us. If, in the daily exercise of free will, we desire the assistance of the Most High, we must command him to descend into our world.

Jesus taught his disciples to pray in the form of short commands by saying, "Thy kingdom come! Thy will be done in earth as it is in heaven!"[3] In fact, the entire Lord's Prayer is a series of commands given by Jesus to the Father.

By consciously uniting our forces with God, by making our will subject to the Divine will and then commanding the Almighty to enter our world and exercise his dominion, we return to him the authority he gave us when he gave the gift of free will.

Meditation and silent prayer are an important part of daily devotions, but dynamic decrees are the most powerful method of directing God's light into the world for individual and planetary change. "Thou shalt also decree a thing and it shall be established unto thee!"[4] is an ancient maxim that sets forth the law governing prayer. For man, created in the image of God, has the self-same power to create that God had "in the beginning" when he said, "Let there be light: and there was light."

Some, accustomed to meditation, may be disturbed at first by praying, or decreeing, aloud. But Lord Maitreya says, "I say to you today that it costs you but a little to try to decree properly and faithfully. Therefore I urge you to understand the meaning of decrees and to practice long enough until you become proficient in establishing through decrees the power of God in your own world.

"How do decrees compare with prayer?" he asks. "Beloved ones, prayer is wonderful, for through prayer as communion with God, the grace of the LORD descends upon the supplicant's heart. But for a vital release of power from the Almighty, prayer is not to be compared with the giving of masterful decrees.

"Various yogic systems of meditation offer methods whereby the mind of man can be stilled and a greater attunement with the Divine be achieved. Some of the methods become haphazard when applied by the Western man, for they do require an advanced mental and spiritual discipline on the part of the one employing them. Decrees, on the other hand, are relatively simple to grasp once the basic principles are understood, and they are far more efficacious."[5]

Saint Germain tells us, "The proper use of decrees takes practice. Individuals should not expect that the first time they make a call, the very perfection of the universe will sweep away all of the accumulated debris of their lives.

"Proper decreeing is an art, and as one gains greater proficiency, he will find it possible to speed up his decrees—that is, he will be able to speed up the rate at which they are given. He will also be able to understand what is taking place as he speeds them up; for this acceleration, by raising the rate of his own electronic pattern, throws off and transmutes the negative thoughts and feelings in his world."[6]

Let us turn now to the science of invocation.

Importance of Invocation

We have discussed how the armies of heaven cannot come to our aid unless we invite them. We are the authority in our octave and the angels and ascended masters cannot enter here unless they are asked to.

Hercules, the Elohim of the First Ray, told us that he had legions of angels and elementals working for him, but they must be called into action by us. No matter how eager they may be to help, they cannot enter our world until we call them.

Mother Mary said, "Remember, beloved ones, you do not need to struggle. The hosts of the Lord are encamped about you and they indeed go forth, and they are the conquerors."

Portia, Goddess of Justice and Opportunity and Saint

Germain's twin flame, once said that she had legions of angels standing on the hillsides, just waiting for our call. They returned to her at the end of the day and said, "Nobody called us. We couldn't do anything."

Perhaps now you can visualize how important your calls are—your prayers, your fiats, your invocations, your decrees. The elemental beings of fire, air, water and earth do not have free will as we do. They are obedient to mankind's wishes—either positive or negative—and need to be given the authority to move into action and help us.

Never forget that God is the doer. It is not your responsibility to fight the battle against darkness. This belongs to the angels and cosmic beings. However, you have an essential part to play in this equation, and your part is to make the calls so that the hosts of heaven can enter your world and fight your battles for you.

Serapis Bey addresses the class saying, "We have only had a short explanation of decrees tonight, but I am assigning for your work at home a tape recording of devotees giving violet flame decrees. In this way you can hear for yourself the rhythm of the decrees.* I can also recommend several books which I should like to have you study to complement the teachings I have given you in the retreat.

"May I close this night with a quotation from the Old Testament," Serapis says. "I can say little more than that which was spoken of old. 'Prove me now herewith, saith the LORD *of hosts, if I will not open you the windows of heaven, and pour you out a blessing that there shall not be room enough to receive it.'*[7]

"Good night, beloved ones."

---

*See bibliography, p. 253.

~If you wish to further enhance your study before proceeding to Chapter 13, you will find exercises on p. 229.

CHAPTER THIRTEEN

❦

Divine Psychology

Serapis Bey begins his class by saying, "I have invited
Lord Lanto to address us tonight on the subject of our psychology with special emphasis on our moods.

"Beloved Lanto is Lord of the Second Ray of Wisdom
and Illumination. An ascended master of great attainment, he
conducts classes for unascended students at the Royal Teton
Retreat in the etheric realms over Wyoming and works closely
with Saint Germain for the freedom of mankind in this age.

"God Meru, Lord Lanto and Kuthumi serve together to
bring the fundamentals of divine psychology again to this age.
Please welcome Lord Lanto."

Lanto begins:.

"Each man's culture is dominated by the patterns that lie
deep within his subconscious being. Frequently men say that
they do not understand themselves. They do not know why
they act as they do. It is not possible for them to open the
doorway of consciousness, to roam the corridors of memory
and to see each habit in its development and then to weed out
each undesirable thought. There is a better way, and that way
is the saturation of the consciousness with the flame of cosmic
worth.

"Even as Archangel Michael and the Lord Christ did not
hesitate in their contentions with evil to say, 'Get thee behind
me,' so the student must not hesitate when he is made aware
of the fact that he is coming under the influence of moods to
rebuke those feelings which are foreign to his true nature. He
must, if he would be freeborn, always control his moods
before they control him." [1]

Moods

We see now that we must learn at all costs to control our moods before they control us. Do you know that all the heaviness you may be feeling at the present moment may not necessarily be your own? The Great Divine Director tells us that currents of negative energy float abroad in the atmosphere and are the accumulations of the mass mind. It may be that they can gain entrance into your world through a slight opening in your subconscious or unconscious mind and cause you to identify with them.

In Genesis we were told to take dominion over the earth, and that can include taking dominion over our thoughts and feelings if we wish to conquer time and space and receive the gift of the ascension. Instead of concentrating on negativity, all we need do is call upon the law of forgiveness, throw all these thoughts into the violet flame and then move forward in the flame of joy.

Passing the flames through the conscious and subconscious mind is a ritual that has been practiced for centuries by devotees of God.

A Change of Pace

Lanto has a solution to the problem of negativity impinging upon the aura—whether from karma coming up for redemption or from the mass consciousness. He says, "Sometimes a change of pace is all that is necessary to prevent the further encroachment of the negative force of the mood upon the psyche."

The Great Divine Director says the same thing in a slightly different way: "When you feel an energy that you can't decree away, remove yourself from the immediate vicinity."

Sometimes it is necessary to get away from where we are, go shopping downtown or walk around the block and look up at the glorious clouds and say, "O God, you are so magnificent." Or we may find a quiet place and take a moment to center in our heart. A change of pace may be all we need to completely clear our consciousness of whatever is troubling us.

This little key has been of more help than anything else when we are beset by energy that leaves us unsure of what to do next. It is the fastest way to clear our forcefield, for what is bothering us may not be our own consciousness but the consciousness of mankind in general.

Floating grids and forcefields, as the Great Divine Director calls them, may be influencing our moods. When people send out waves of disturbed emotions, such as fear, hatred, condemnation, resentment, rebellion, anger or jealousy, these emotions form clouds of energy that may settle on us and cause us to feel moody.

Often, as Lanto tells us, "time is needed for the four lower bodies to recover from the influence of moods. When the consciousness is overwhelmed by moods of anger, fear, grief, resentment or a general feeling of irritation, there is an invasion of psychic substance that is completely foreign to the soul. The soul must, therefore, be given time to throw off this substance, and this is effected in much the same manner as the physical body expels toxins."[2]

Call to Archangel Michael's Sword of Blue Flame

These substances must be changed into light if our planet is to continue its progress, for these vibrations prey upon people and cause them to be depressed and unhappy without realizing why. Take courage! Call to Archangel Michael and his angelic hosts and ask for his spiritual sword of blue flame to blaze into these conditions daily as you give your dynamic decrees.

After taking a little time out, come back and continue whatever you were doing and you'll find that things go much better. We've been told that we can become entrapped in the discord that millions of people each day pour out toward one another over the cities and throughout the entire planet.

Serapis thanks Lord Lanto for this information and says that he would now like us to hear from the Ascended Master Kuthumi for the remainder of our time tonight.

Many knew and worked with Kuthumi in the Middle Ages when he was known as Saint Francis, the founder of the Franciscan Order of monks. Many of us took vows with him of poverty, chastity and obedience. He is our master psychologist and sponsor of youth. Kuthumi serves today with Jesus in the office of World Teacher and is responsible for setting forth in the two-thousand-year cycle of the Piscean age the teachings which will lead to individual self-mastery and the Christ Consciousness.

Kuthumi is dressed in the brown habit girdled at the waist with rope that many of us remember from our lives as Franciscan monks. He will teach on one of his favorite subjects: the aura.

Keep Your Aura Filled with Light

Kuthumi tells us that our aura needs protection from the impinging vibrations of mankind, so here is a visualization that will help you seal your aura against oncoming energy. When you walk down the street, see your aura so completely filled with light that it surrounds you like a big balloon.

The light filling your aura is so completely impenetrable that one of two things happens: either the mass consciousness with all its negative vibrations rushes against you and then bounces right back again, or your aura is so filled with the violet flame that you immediately transmute all the projections that come your way.

Unfortunately, most people have allowed their auric balloons to become concave. This means that the aura is caved in instead of being puffed out with light. Some can become exhausted when their aura has absorbed negative energy and often they do not know how to get rid of it.

The answer is that we have not filled our aura with enough light. We need to protect the light in our aura by our calls for our tube of light and by our calls to Archangel Michael.

Call for legions of angels to encircle you with drawn swords. Tell Lord Michael to place his blue-flame angels around you so that you won't feel tired, so that in addition to your daily work you will have enough energy to contribute to the masters.

The best exercise is to see yourself with your aura so bright that projections just bounce right off it. Then your cycle of mood swings—from depression to bliss to normalcy and back again—is over. We've all been caught in this for thousands of years, but now is the time to stay positive and to remain in the flame of harmony and good humor in order to make our ascension.

Need for Protection

Here is a simple mantra we can say hundreds of times a day until our aura glows blue with Archangel Michael's flame of protection. Visualize Archangel Michael and his legions of blue-flame angels surrounding us, defeating and turning back all that assails us.

We should be sure to give this prayer as traveling protection before we drive our car or enter public transportation:

> Lord Michael before, Lord Michael behind,
> Lord Michael to the right,
> Lord Michael to the left,
> Lord Michael above, Lord Michael below,
> Lord Michael, Lord Michael wherever I go!
>
> I AM his love protecting here!
> I AM his love protecting here!
> I AM his love protecting here!

Here is Kuthumi's excellent visualization to free you from feeling down on yourself. Say aloud, "Today I am a focus of the Central Sun. Flowing through me is a crystal river of light." See and feel yourself as a great Niagara of light. Again, say, "I AM an outpost of the Divine. Such darkness as has used me is swallowed up by the mighty river of light which I AM."

When you accept this, your gloom will be swiftly washed away. A river of light is descending from God through your crystal cord—from your I AM Presence, down into your three-fold flame anchored in your heart—and it will flush out all darkness in you if you let it.

Carry this little decree in your purse or pocket and take it out whenever problems assail you. You will soon find that you have memorized it and eventually it will sing through your mind continually. You can call it up whenever you need a reinforcement of light—a shot in the arm, as it were.

I AM Light
by Kuthumi

I AM light, glowing light,
Radiating light, intensified light.
God consumes my darkness,
Transmuting it into light.

This day I AM a focus of the Central Sun.
Flowing through me is a crystal river,
A living fountain of light
That can never be qualified
By human thought and feeling.
I AM an outpost of the Divine.
Such darkness as has used me is swallowed up
By the mighty river of light which I AM.

I AM, I AM, I AM light;
I live, I live, I live in light.
I AM light's fullest dimension;
I AM light's purest intention.
I AM light, light, light
Flooding the world everywhere I move,
Blessing, strengthening and conveying
The purpose of the kingdom of heaven.[3]

If you have a difficult time visualizing, find a picture of a beautiful waterfall and keep it before you as you give this decree. See this great waterfall of light sweeping away all darkness in your life, all rebellion, all depression, all fear, all disbelief, all that is bothering you at the moment. Repeat this decree over and over and over again until you feel relief.

If you can maintain the image of yourself as a river of light, a great waterfall of light that swallows up any darkness coming your way, you will have a much easier time as you progress up the path to your ascension.

Kuthumi leaves us with a greeting that inspires hope in all of us. He says, "Farewell for the moment, my beloved heart friends of the ages. I hope to greet you soon as ascended masters. Keep striving, because this is a very present possibility for all of you."

◦If you wish to further enhance your study before proceeding to Chapter 14, you will find exercises on p. 229.

CHAPTER FOURTEEN

❧

Your Christhood

Serapis greets us today with an assignment he gives to all his classes of initiates in the retreat at Luxor. Recently, he has begun to teach this exercise to students at Summit University in Montana.

An Assignment from Serapis

Serapis has assigned us to keep a book called *My Christhood* that has two separate columns for notes. One column is for listing the virtues we believe we have already and the second one is for listing the faults we *know* we have. As we progress in our spiritual evolution and our attunement with our Christ Self, we will want to look back often and see how many of the negative qualities we listed have been changed to positive ones.

Serapis has told us that if there could be a vibration of jealousy or envy among candidates for the ascension at Luxor, it would be because we, the students in this class, have a greater opportunity to work out our karma in a physical body than the candidates in the retreats who are in their etheric body between embodiments.

It takes ten times longer to balance karma in an etheric body and only a certain type of karma can be balanced there. So even though the candidates at Luxor may have passed all their tests and learned all their lessons, they must embody again to balance their karma on earth.

The Assignment on Our Christhood

Serapis turns to us and says:

"Seriously consider this day and hour your opportunity to be in a human body to 'work out your salvation,' as Paul said, 'with fear and trembling'[1] but I say with joy and triumph and

with discipline and devotion. *You have the opportunity to win both by love and by wisdom, infused with the power of the spoken Word.*

"Let us begin our assignment. *The real miracle and the first lesson of alchemy at Luxor is the separating out of the Real from the unreal in the being of the individual. What is real in you? What is unreal?*

"*I charge you to begin your book this day, students of the Most High God; for you are not students of Serapis Bey or Morya or Saint Germain, but you are students of the Almighty, of the Christ. And we, the ascended masters, stand as mentors and fellow servants of the Most High God.*

"*I charge you then, this day, to take a page in your book of Christhood and to make two columns. The first column is about myself, what is Real—the second column concerns myself, what is unreal.*

"*You will head the first column with the words,* God, the I AM THAT I AM; Christ the Only Begotten Son, *for this is that which is real within you.*

"*You will head the second column with* The human ego, the human will, the human intellect, the human pride.

"*And then you will list in the first column the virtues of the light, the virtues of the Christ and of God that you know to be real and to be outpictured within you. And in the second, you will list those faults and sins that are not real.*

"*Then you will return to the first column and list the attributes that you desire to have real, that you know exist, that you know and adore but have not yet mastered. These you will also claim as your Self, as Reality. For unless and until you claim them, you cannot be them.*

"*Thus you will clearly mark the truth and the falsehood of identity. This is the starting place of the ascension. That which is in the first column must rise; that which is in the second must be transmuted before it can rise.*

"*Then step by step each day, with rejoicing in your heart, you take the power, the dominion of the God qualities you have listed in the first column and all energies that you have listed there. Then you use them as your authority, your substance, your collateral to invoke the grace of God, his will and his healing to remove the stain of sin and all unreality that you have listed in the second column.*

"This, then, becomes an objective and practical exercise in the demonstration of the science of the laws of God.[2]

"When you systematize the path to the ascension, you set before you what must be overcome by light. You set before you the incorruptible nature of man and the corruptible nature. And you know that by divine decree the corruptible man must now put on incorruption.

"You must be alchemists of the first degree. You must practice the science of alchemy, of changing the base metals of the human consciousness into the gold of the Christ consciousness. This you do in the name of Jesus the Christ, in the name of Saint Germain, in the name of El Morya and in the name of Mother Mary. This you do in the name of all who have become the Christ, in the name of the overcoming spirit of victory of all the saints and ascended beings and the heavenly hosts of all ages.

"You must make the effort. You must be systematic. You must have a daily ritual you practice in defense of your divinity. And if you come knocking on the doors of Luxor seeking entrance, you will gain that entrance more easily than you will retain the admittance. For we do not allow students to remain at Luxor who do not show the devotion of self-discipline that is required to pursue the ascension currents.

"I say again, this is the starting place of the ascension. That which is in the first column must rise. That which is in the second must be transmuted before it can rise. Keep on, valiant ones. Lose not the sight for a moment of the ultimate goal while also keeping your vision upon the present, for we shall prevail by unity with God and with one another."

We Resolve to Complete the Exercise

As we meditate on the master's words, we realize that to enter into the vibration of self-condemnation can negate the value of this entire exercise. As we make this list of our virtues and our faults, we must realize that we are still in the process of overcoming. If we were perfected, we would already be ascended and have no need for Serapis Bey's assignment!

So we must keep these lists before us as a goal to enable us to gradually transmute the unreal into the Real. We must sincerely make invocations to the masters and to God to help us, for in that way we will be surprised how soon we can transmute our negative character traits into the reality of our Christhood.

Transmuting the negative into the positive is one of the most important aspects of the whole exercise. If we have listed very few qualities in the first column and a long laundry list of faults in the second column, we are not yet claiming our Christhood. We are still saying, "Lord, I am not worthy." We must throw all our feelings of inadequacy into the violet flame and look upon ourselves with the eyes of the Christ.

With strength itself we shall overcome because God wills it so. Our ascension is God's desire for us.

Lanello's Assignment

We have a second assignment for our Christhood book and this time the assignment is from the Ascended Master Lanello.

Mark Prophet was our teacher until his passing in 1973. He remembered the problems in his own life and this assignment has been an offering from his heart as the Ascended Master Lanello. Since he was so recently among us, Lanello has insights to give us that he knows will help us.

He has been a great friend throughout the ages and has been with us in many of his embodiments. You may feel his flame as Lanello even if you did not know him as Mark Prophet in this life.

Mark and Elizabeth Prophet are twin flames who dedicated their lives to serving as messengers for the ascended masters. They agreed to receive dictations—messages from the masters received while in a heightened state of awareness.

In order to be messengers of God in this age, both Mark and Elizabeth have had many lives of preparation, and in this life have served as teachers, lecturers, writers and the founders of The Summit Lighthouse. Later they opened Summit University as another organization through which the masters could teach devotees on the path to the ascension.

Mark Prophet made his ascension on February 26, 1973, and now continues to serve as the Ascended Master Lanello. He works closely with El Morya and other masters of the Darjeeling Council. His own retreat is over the Rhine River in Germany.

Lanello steps to the lectern and says, "Yes, dear hearts, I see several who knew me as Mark. I am eager for the day when I can greet you as ascended masters. Perhaps that day will not be too far off.

"Here is my assignment. Take up your book My Christhood *and add another section after Serapis' assignment. In this new section, start a diary that is called your* Christhood Diary.

"Write down each day how the flower of the Christ is appearing in your life. And when you know you have done an act in the consciousness of the Christ, write it down and leave the record for yourself so that in those hours of darkness and moments of trial when you forget and cannot remember one good thing you have ever done because the devils are tormenting you with their lies, read in your diary how you have vanquished error and how you have overcome.

"There is no need to tarry; there is no need to go back to the old ways of the human consciousness. I say, your Christed awareness, your Christed Being, is the blazing reality of your consciousness! It is the new day dawning within you! It is your potential of victory! It is your purity now!

"And I say, you do not have to wait for that carnal mind

to evolve, for the carnal mind will never evolve, precious hearts. It will never become the Christ. It must be put off and cast into the flame! You have to trade in the old model and take out the new.

"How long will you dwell with that old model? Some of you are more tolerant of your former selves than you are of your cars that you trade in every year, but you forget to trade in the carnal mind for the Christ Mind that is in the height of fashion in the courts of heaven!

"And so, precious hearts, I say that of all of the warnings and all of the prophecies that I might prophesy, it is this one key of Christhood, and salvation through Christhood, that can give you the ultimate victory. And it is with ultimate victories that we are concerned—not with the skirmishes that are lost or won each hour and each day!"

Forgive Yourself

This was the first gift that Mark gave us after his ascension as Lanello. He was a Capricorn, and so in addition to his own self-condemnation that he had to overcome, he was holding the balance for all the planetary condemnation on the 12 o'clock line of the cosmic clock.* He knew so well that there are days when we can't think of a single thing we've ever done that is of use to this world.

That's why Lanello would say: "If a thought comes to you in your meditation, if you find a little gem in a devotional book—write it down! And then when the devils are tormenting you, open your book and there in black and white are the good things you have done." He wants us to be able to arrest that spiral of self-condemnation right then and there and say, "Well now, things aren't so bad after all! There is still some hope for me!"

We may also call to the Great Divine Director, who knows how to arrest spirals and initiate new ones, saying, "In the name of my I AM Presence, I command that this spiral of negativity be

*See workbook, p. 233 and glossary, p. 246.

arrested and by the power of my God Presence I ask you to initiate a new spiral of God-victory."

We can call to Lanello to break old habits and start new ones—first to throw them out of our lives and then to replace them. The way to break a bad habit is to completely replace it with a good one.

Many times, El Morya has told us, "From the beginning we were winning." Now, we have lost some battles, there is no doubt about it, but we will win the war.

Keep in mind, however, that skirmishes count. We have a cosmic bookkeeper, the great Keeper of the Scrolls, who marks on his computer what we do each day with each erg of energy God has given us. But when we stumble, as we will occasionally because we are not yet perfected, we should apologize to God, ask him to forgive our errors and then cast them into the violet flame, call upon the law of forgiveness and move on.

Be concerned about your actions but do not criticize, condemn and belittle yourself. That is as detrimental as condemning others, for you are condemning the spark of God within you, and you are actually practicing witchcraft and black magic against yourself.

Sometimes, as Lanello tells us, when we lose in the fray, it is because we need to learn a lesson from it. And a temporary loss may mean an ultimate victory, for a lesson gained is a measure toward perfection. Often when we fail at something, we learn more from it than from our successes.

We should take the time to assess ourselves and see what we have done wrong, and then make sure that we don't repeat our error. We can then count the experiences we have had as the past that is prologue to a future success. In other words, we made a mistake, we're sorry. And now, we will move on to victory.

Remember El Morya's quote, "Do not then decry the fact that you must of necessity make some mistakes, nor remain upon the ground when you fall or stumble. Arise at once and proceed onward."

Don't keep rehashing all those old memories. You can become involved in revolving past scenes by saying, "I wish I hadn't done that. Well, since I did that, now what am I going to do?" Instead, you should just say, "LORD, send the violet flame through me." Then forgive yourself and try harder tomorrow.

Lanello would say that the saga of many of our lives is beautiful to behold, for we have indeed won in small ways and in great ways. And until the last tally is taken, we will never know how the LORD looks upon us. All we see and know is our present span of life.

We have lived for thousands and thousands of years. We have been both men and women. We have been paupers. We have been wealthy. We have known lives of degradation and lives of sainthood. We are a conglomerate of all our lives up until now and we have experienced various phases of life that we cannot even remember at present.

In our Causal Body we have much good stored that may be completely unknown to us until we are shown our past lives by the masters or until the moment of our ascension. So when we feel that we are certainly not very important and don't count for very much, we are seeing just this one little speck on the line of our whole evolution.

All our many good embodiments are written in our book of life in heaven, even if we are not aware of them at this moment. The mercy of reincarnation is that we are allowed to come back again and are given a chance to correct our mistakes.

To sum it up. If you have a record of your victories in your *Christhood Diary,* you will have something to sustain you on days when you are depressed. It is interesting to note that one's good experiences are fleeting experiences. They vanish from our memory. Often we totally forget all the good we have experienced with each other and with God.

So unless we have a record of our experiences, we can go through life oblivious of the golden moments, the moments of love and communion. Because they are behind us, they blend into one another. And then in the hour of temptation we have nothing to help us bolster our faith and make us remember, "Why yes, God did appear to me. God did speak to me. Yes, I felt his radiation. Yes, I was initiated. Yes, I will remember and keep on keeping on."

As he concludes his teaching for the night, Lanello leaves us with a word of comfort:

"When you are going through that hour of trial and decision to be or not to be in God, if you can read your personal diary of your experiences with God, there's no question that you will pass your test.

"So keep on striving for the light, striving for the right. And know that I, Lanello, walk with you each step of the way."

~ *If you wish to further enhance your study before proceeding to Chapter 15, you will find exercises on p. 232.*

CHAPTER FIFTEEN

❦

The Electronic Presence of a Master

*O*ur guest tonight is Mother Mary," Serapis announces. *"If you have been Catholic, you may know her as the Blessed Virgin, the Blessed Mother, the Mother of God. She was the mother of Jesus Christ in his Galilean embodiment and she is the twin flame of Archangel Raphael. She and Raphael bear the flame of healing to souls who are in pain. Although Mary is an archeai, she took embodiment as a physical woman for many years before she ascended back to the archangel's realm. She has appeared at Fátima, Lourdes and many other places in the past and is still appearing all over the world to the faithful—including this class this evening."*

Mother Mary begins her instruction:

"Beloved ones, I would like to tell you about the Electronic Presence of a master tonight. If you could reach out your hand and touch mine, you would almost feel that there is very little between us. Very fine is the line between the angelic hosts and mankind. As you give your prayers, as you are in your beds at night, realize that simply by a touch, by a thought, by a point of light we are in your presence.

"Ask that the Electronic Presence of the master of your choice be superimposed over your form before you go to sleep at night. You will find that throughout the hours of rest all the momentums of light of that ascended being can be absorbed into your consciousness, into your four lower bodies.

"Realize what this can mean for you ere you go to sleep at night. Say, 'Beloved Father, beloved Jesus the Christ, send me the Electronic Presence of yourself and let that duplicate of your image rest over me and through me and in me while

my body sleeps.' You will waken, then, with the spirit of the
resurrection flame within you as Christ awakened on Easter
morning. You will find that you have within you the full pulsation of that mighty flame that is his full-gathered momentum of the victory of the ascension currents.

"Do you see what this can mean to you if systematically
you make a list for yourself of all the known members of the
hierarchy? and then each night call to a different master,
make supplication to the flame on which he serves, and then
ask for that to be imbibed by you.

"You will, then, be given mighty assistance that otherwise
might take many generations for you to develop through your
own inner training and through the application of your own
heart flame without the assistance of the momentum of the
beings of light."[1]

A Duplicate of the Master's I AM Presence

To know how to ask for the Electronic Presence of a master to
be placed over you is one of the greatest keys you can have
toward your ascension. The Electronic Presence of an ascended
master is a duplicate of his God Presence. Thus, instead of
having to master all of life yourself by trial and error, you can
have access to the master's momentum of attainment.

Each master has his own particular flame; each has overcome in a different way. If you feel you need more willpower, call
for El Morya's Presence over you as you sleep. If you desire more
purity, call to Serapis Bey and the Goddess of Purity. If you feel
a lack of wisdom or illumination, call to Kuthumi.

If you form the habit of calling for the master's Presence over
you as you sleep, you will soon find that you will awaken with
insights and ideas that are invaluable. By using this dispensation
diligently, you can cut years off the time necessary to become a
candidate for the ascension. The masters can teach your soul
more easily while the body is at rest and you are not distracted
by the many tasks of everyday life.

The Ascended Masters Are Omnipresent

Lest you feel selfish about calling to El Morya or Serapis Bey or Lanello or Jesus, afraid to disturb them when they may have some important cosmic work to do, you should know that since they are one with God, they are omnipresent.

Thousands of people throughout the world can call to Jesus and he can send his Electronic Presence to each one and yet still maintain his own oneness with the Father. You may call for the Electronic Presence of Lanello to be placed over you without in any way detracting from his own service to the light.

A thorough understanding of the Electronic Presence of a master is vital to an initiate on the Path. Remember, it is a duplicate of the master's I AM Presence. Realize that an ascended being can be everywhere he is needed at any given moment.

You can call to Jesus, I can call to Jesus, someone in Africa can call to Jesus, and he can respond to each one. He can project his Presence a thousand or a million times over to each one who needs him and still continue with his own work.

So don't feel that you are disturbing the masters by asking them to be with you. In fact, they hope that you will call to them often so that they can help you. Mother Mary has told us, "If you could realize how little is the distance that separates us! If you could just stand on tiptoe, you would almost bump into the ascended masters' realm!"

I would like to tell you about one of the dispensations that Lanello has offered us. He has offered us his Electronic Presence during the daytime, so we are now able to live twenty-four hours a day with his Presence over us. Thus we can call for the Presence of a master as we go to sleep at night and we can call for Lanello to walk with us during the day. We may choose to live in the aura of an ascended master constantly.

Those of us who knew Mark Prophet when he was with us know that his love for all of us is now even greater than when he was hampered by his body. He is completely free as the Ascended Master Lanello, and he can be with us any time we call to him.

He has said, "I am as near as the breath that you breathe. And there is nowhere that you can go that I am not, for I have projected an Electronic Presence of myself to each one of you who will receive me.

"And so we two shall walk hand in hand, and at any hour of the day or night when you reach out your hand for mine, I will clasp your own."

When things get rough, if you will say, "Beloved I AM Presence, beloved Lanello, help me!" That is all it takes. That is all he is asking for—just a quick, "Lanello, help. Lanello, please come."

Lanello Will Sponsor You

He has also told us, "I say, you are all candidates for the ascension if you choose to be. And if you choose to be this night and in the coming weeks, then I will sponsor you and I will direct the Mother of the Flame to sponsor you also."

That means Lanello will stand before Serapis Bey and the Lords of Karma and say, "I will stand as sponsor for this lifestream in case he does not have quite enough attainment or enough karma balanced to warrant being a candidate for the ascension and receive the teachings of the ascended masters."

He will pledge part of his light, like a co-signer at the bank if you do not have enough collateral. But also, as happens when you sign a note for someone, he must say, "If this person defects, I will give part of my attainment to make up for it." Can you imagine the depth of love an ascended master has to make an offer like that?

Lanello liked to joke about the name that was his before his ascension—Mark Prophet. He said, "As Jesus wrote, 'He that receiveth a Prophet in the name of a Prophet shall receive a Prophet's reward.'[2] My reward is the ascension! My reward is light!

"And if you will receive me as a prophet of your ascension, then you can have my Electronic Presence walking next to you, and I will wear my own blue cape and they will say, 'Look at those twins walking down the street.' For you will look like me and I will look like you and who will say who is ascended and who is unascended? For did they not have a little moment of trouble discerning the difference between Jesus and his disciples?

"So they will not know who is who. And I dare say that when the negative forces move their chessmen on the board of life to attack your lifestream, they may very well fling those arrows of outrageous fortune at me! And then they will have the reward of attacking an ascended master! And how do you like that?"

God bless our Lanello! He really loves us!

A word about Lanello's blue cape that he has offered us to wear as we walk down the street with him. Mark used to wear a beautiful sapphire-blue cape whenever he took dictations from a blue-ray master. When he stepped on the platform wearing his blue cape, you could just feel the blue lightning crackle and know that there would be a dictation from El Morya, Archangel Michael or the Great Divine Director.

If we can make a habit of living twenty-four hours a day within the aura of an ascended master, we will find that a lot of our problems disappear. This is one of the most vital keys to our Christhood.

⊱If you wish to further enhance your study before proceeding to Chapter 16, you will find exercises on p. 232.

❦

CHAPTER SIXTEEN

Understanding Yourself

Serapis tells us that he has invited the three ascended master psychologists, Kuthumi, Lanto and Meru, to be present as a panel of guest lecturers later in the evening. But first he has a few things he wants us to know concerning the way we learn to understand ourselves.

Man, Know Thyself as God

Have you ever contemplated a Self beyond the self? By pursuing the study of divine psychology, you can find your Real Self. For although it seems real, the appearance world is a world of illusion. To some even the idiosyncrasies of the human personality take on a form of reality whereas in truth only the Self is real.

We need to first understand ourselves and then to learn how to rule ourselves. In Genesis we given dominion "over all the earth." [1] Thus we need to shatter the chains that bind us to conditions of unhappiness and strain, often unknowingly created by ourselves, and take dominion over our lives to find the Reality that we seek.

The inscription on the ancient temples of the East, "Man know thyself," was intended to say, "Man, know thyself as God." For when we know ourselves as God, we will have overcome our human state. We need to go back to the full meaning of this inscription to remove much of the insecurity and low self-esteem prevalent among us today.

Similarly, we have forgotten the words of the Psalmist to the Israelites: "Ye are gods; and all of you are children of the most High." [2] Moses exhorted the children of Israel to "choose life," [3] not death. To choose the ascension in the light is to choose eternal life. It is our victorious return to the Father when we have overcome our lower nature.

We Are Sons and Daughters of God

The answer to many of the bewildering questions we face today, lies in our acceptance of the fact that we are sons and daughters of God. We must believe in, rejoice in and accept the Father's proffered gift of our ascension! For we have the choice to remain snarled in the nets of our karma or to exercise our God-given right to freedom from these trials. It is entirely up to us.

Mastering our lower self and directing our energies to our Higher Self requires us to pass initiations along the way. In fact, one of the most difficult initiations we may have to pass is understanding ourselves—understanding who we are, why we do the things we do and what the purpose of life is.

Saint Paul said, "For the good that I would, I do not; but the evil which I would not, that I do."[4] And at times many of us feel exactly like Paul.

Be Ye in the World but Not of It

Jesus wanted us to be in the world but not of it. Contemplating this, we realize that we have all had lifetimes where we were yogis, saints or sages, who lived lives of contemplation in seclusion from the world. But in this life we must demonstrate our mastery in the cities, in the workplace, in the home, amidst everyday situations and problems. We need to find our way out of our problems and reach up to a higher realm of divine happiness and joy while still living in the cities of the world.

I have often thought that the battle we are fighting today— this personal battle of Armageddon between our lower and our higher natures, between our ego and our carnal mind, between the forces of light and the forces of darkness—is much more difficult now than at any other time in history.

In other lifetimes we have fought physical battles where we could see the enemy. Our foe stood in front of us. We could see him and we could load our musket and fire at him. We could do something physical, tangible.

Now we can't. But we're fighting this battle of Armageddon nonetheless, perhaps even more so than in the American Revolution or the French Revolution or any of the wars throughout history. But we can't see the enemy.

We are fighting against witchcraft, against energies coming up from our electronic belt, our carnal mind, world karma, and we can't see a thing. We don't know why we feel the way we do. Surely it would be easier to stand with George Washington in the snow at Valley Forge!

But the battle must be fought and the battle must be won. It's not a physical battle now. It's primarily an astral, mental and emotional one—although it can be very physical at times, as we see in Bosnia, Kosovo, Iraq and many other countries.

However, we can fight this battle. And <u>we can fight it with the science of the spoken Word as our ammunition.</u> We must take up our decree book, give some dynamic decrees and fiats and ask Archangel Michael and the hosts of the LORD to enter the fray and help us defeat these unseen forces.

<u>All of Heaven</u> is eager to come to our assistance. But as we said before, <u>we must invoke</u> the angels and the masters and give them permission to enter our world. Our prayers, decrees, fiats, invocations—these are our bullets in the present-day battle of Armageddon.

Peace, Be Still!

Mother Mary has come with some excellent instruction on how to "take dominion over the earth." She says: "The soft voice, the gentle whisper of the Holy Spirit, is the only presence of the creative force of life within you. The holding to and clinging fast to that vine of divinity will work wonders in the world of form for you.

"And whenever you are amidst the tempest, as beloved Jesus was in the boat and the sea roared without, remember

that you can simply say, 'Peace, be still, and know that I AM
God!' And you can call to your I AM Presence, the entire
Spirit of the Great White Brotherhood or an individual
ascended being and say, 'Mighty I AM Presence, take command of that situation!' and know that all will be well. Then,
turn your attention to God and go about your daily activities.

"Do not feel that you must strive alone with opposition.
The forces of light, the power of Michael's band and of all
the archangels stand ready to go forth to do battle for you as
you continue to press forward toward the mark of the high
calling in Christ Jesus.[5]

"Prepare for troublesome situations by having simple
little calls like these right at hand.

'Peace be still and know that I am God.'

'God is my victory!'

'Beloved Saint Germain, You take command of this entire
situation, I shall not be moved!'

'I am a being of violet fire!'

'Be gone, forces of anti-love!'

'If God be for us, who can be against us?'[6]

'God is Love!'

'I AM Presence, thou art master,

'I AM Presence clear the way!'

'I can do all things through Christ which strengtheneth
me!'[7]

"You must realize that when you are caught in a struggle,
you have the ability to immediately rise above it. But first you
have to make the call to allow the masters and angels to come
into your world."

The Golden Mean

Let us turn to the path of the Buddha. He demonstrated the
golden mean, the Middle Way, neither of asceticism nor of
opulence, for Gautama Buddha experienced both in his life as
Siddhartha.

He was born in a palace. His father was a ruler who gave his son every luxury, every indulgence. Siddhartha was kept from seeing poverty, illness—all the sadness of the world. He had a beautiful young wife and a young son. He led a life of wealth and pleasure, and that was all he knew.

One day, you remember the story, he went out on his own and suddenly saw an old man, a diseased man, a dead man and a holy man. And he decided that there must be more to life than the way he had been living.

So he left his palace and went wandering for years in the forest, attaching himself to groups of monks and living a life of great asceticism. He ate practically nothing and almost died of starvation; he did not bathe or allow himself any indulgence, for it was a life of complete renunciation.

Suddenly he realized that this was not the way to enlightenment. Through meditation he understood that the way to attainment was the middle way—the path of nonattachment. In this way one would not be attached to poverty or to riches, to happiness or to unhappiness. He saw that desire brings us unhappiness.

However, he knew that we must retain a certain amount of desire. We must become well-rounded individuals if we plan to progress on the Path. We must desire our ascension, but within reasonable limits. Inordinate attachment to anything defeats our purpose.

The fanatical pursuit of any desire is not the ascended masters' way. We are meant to live in the world. We are meant to keep our bodies healthy and to eat good food. We are not meant to be food fanatics, to diet to excess, to work our bodies too much. We are meant to have the Buddha's nonattachment, his golden mean, the Middle Way.

Nonattachment

Nonattachment is another initiation on the path to the ascension—a test many of us have a difficult time passing. It's a matter of our attitude, how we perceive things, how we react to things.

Lanto says, "Attitude is all-important, for it is like a screen through which the ingredients of life are pressed. What comes out as the individual's life is molded by his attitude."

Remember the optimist and the pessimist? One sees the doughnut, the other the hole. One sees the glass half full, the other sees it half empty. What's the difference? Attitude!

Some parents have a difficult time allowing their children to grow up and live their own lives, for they try to live their lives vicariously through their children. Many of us left home because our souls recognized that we could not allow someone else to control our lives. Such parents need to work with the Buddha on nonattachment to the fruit of action.

They must realize that their role is to give life to the child, to train the child in the ways of love and righteousness during the formative years. Later, their role changes. They must still pray for their adult children, but it is time to love them and let them go.

A professor in educational psychology once said, "The prime purpose of a parent is to teach his child to be independent and then to give him that independence. That is the difficult part— the letting go."

Each of us must be set free to make our own mistakes and learn by them. Striving is just as important as succeeding. If you have done the best you possibly can and then things go wrong and are out of your control, don't sit there and condemn yourself. Accept that you may be experiencing the initiation of nonattachment to the fruit of action.

Turn to something positive. Hear the words "God is my victory, victory, victory. God is my victory, victory, victory," echoing to the click of your heels as you walk along all day. Pretty soon, as you form the habit of accepting positive keys into your world, you will find that there's not room enough for both the negative and the positive. The positive will flush out the negative if you allow it to.

Replace negative thoughts with thoughts of victory. That is the way to ascend daily. It is important that we gain control of our thoughts and our life. No one else can do it for us. The ascension is an ongoing process of being vigilant and diligent about everything that comes to us.

Serapis Bey sees a hand raised in the back of the room and asks for questions and comments.

One student says, "I was privileged to know an older woman who was near her ascension. She had her eyes so fixed on the Christ that the little irritations of everyday life just didn't bother her. Time and time again I heard her mumbling under her breath, 'What is that to me? I will follow thee.'

"She had taken to heart the admonishment of the Christ, 'What is that to thee? Follow thou me.'[8] *Whenever anything would happen to her that would upset other people, she would just say these words to rise above the situation. She had her eye upon her ascension and the irritations of life were not important enough for her to spend her time thinking about. She was a great joy to know and I learned important lessons from her."*

"Thank you," Serapis says. "I know this soul and she did indeed make her ascension. We can all learn an important lesson from her example."

Family Mesmerism

The other side of the coin of parents' attachment to adult children is adult children who hang on to their parents. They are so attached that they refuse to forge an independent life for themselves, either out of fear of facing life or a misguided sense of love for their parents.

Don't misunderstand me. You definitely owe a debt of gratitude to your parents who gave you life. The Bible tells us to "Honor thy father and thy mother."[9] We need to pray for our parents, visit them, love them, but we should not make them the excuse for not living our own life and fulfilling our own divine plan.

The time may come when we should move away from home,

from family and friends. We may be meant to be an Aquarian in this lifetime, to be an ascended master student. Many of our parents are Pisceans. They took embodiment under Jesus and they pledged to be loyal to his flame. Between this life and the next, many will be taught in the retreats and return as Aquarians, ready to walk the path to their ascension.

Serapis looks around the class and says, "I would like to take a minute to ask anyone who has anything to say on the subject of trying to control children or parents to come forward and tell us about your experience."

One woman replies, "I am one of the fortunate ones. I knew Mark Prophet in physical embodiment before he became the Ascended Master Lanello. I learned the lesson you are describing when Mark Prophet once came to our home.

"My father had been a heart patient for many years. We lived in Denver, Colorado in 1930 and his doctor said that if we went to either coast he could probably live six more months, but if we remained in Denver at a high altitude, he would die in six weeks. So we moved to Los Angeles and he passed away in 1968. His six months was extended to 38 years!

"He was a very devout man, a good Christian and I had an orthodox upbringing. We always went to the fundamentalist church, whatever denomination it was, wherever we moved. My father was very close to Jesus so I thought that when he found out about the ascended masters, he would move right along with me.

"I spent many hours explaining the teachings to him but because of his fundamentalist beliefs, he could not understand reincarnation. When I found that Mark Prophet was coming to visit, I increased the tempo of explaining the teachings to my father because I had decided that he must be ready. I could see no reason, since he loved Jesus, why he would not accept the other masters.

"When Mark arrived, I said, 'May we please have a barbecue tonight? I'll invite my father and all my family and

*you explain the teachings to them.' I had spent two years try-
ing to explain reincarnation and I felt there must be something
that I was not explaining correctly. Mark consented and set
forth the entire teachings of the ascended masters, basically
and simply.*

"My father had recently been in the hospital, and by
eleven o'clock that evening I knew he had to go back to bed.
I said, 'Now, Daddy, do you understand?' And he said, 'Oh,
yes indeed! But, Mark, I want to ask you one more question
before I go home.

"'My daughter said that you were Mark in the Bible and
that is my favorite book. But how could you have written it
and still be sitting here tonight in my daughter's backyard?'

"Mark just put his arms around him and said, 'Go to bed,
dear heart. God bless you.'

"Then Mark took me aside and gave me a stern lecture.
He said, 'Young lady, you leave your father alone. He's a very
good man and he's very close to Jesus. He has excellent
karma. He's following the path that he took embodiment on.
He vowed he would uphold Jesus' church and he has. The fact
that he doesn't know Saint Germain is not going to hurt him
in the least.

"'You tell your father at the right time that he is not
going to that Baptist hell he is so afraid of. Tell him that Jesus
is waiting for him with open arms and has a position for him
in the new age.'

"Mark told me to tell my father that all he had to do the
next time he was not feeling well was to say, 'Father, into thy
hands I commend my spirit,'[10] and Jesus would take him.
About six weeks later he was in the hospital again and I said,
'Daddy, I want to tell you what Mark told me.' When I finished, he said, 'You mean I'm not going to hell?' I said, 'No,
you're not going to hell.'

"The next day he passed on.

"I am telling you this because Mark wanted me to know

that there may be some elderly people whose mission this lifetime may not be to follow Saint Germain. My father was working with Jesus up until the last minute. And so for many of you who are worrying about your parents, remember, they may be old Pisceans and they will come back again as new little Aquarians. They don't need to know and accept reincarnation this lifetime—their souls know."

At this point the three psychologists, Kuthumi, Lanto and Meru enter the room. Serapis greets them and then goes on to explain that the remainder of the class will be a free-flowing discussion of various aspects of divine psychology.

Energy Can Neither Be Created Nor Destroyed

First, we must say that no discussion on divine psychology would be complete without an explanation of energy. We have taken God's vibrant, pure energy and used it either rightly or wrongly. If wrongly, either in this or past lives, then it has remained with us as dense substance packed in our electronic belt and in our subconscious and unconscious minds. If we are seriously on the path to the ascension, we are now in the process of transmuting this substance into its original purity.

However, we need help. If we will just say, "O God, help me do this, for I don't know how to do it alone. I'm not strong enough to do it myself, but I want to change my world." That's a start.

Lord Lanto has told us how to clear the electronic belt. He said: "Beneath the surface calm there lies within the consciousness of men much that is undesirable, much that represents the polarization of imperfection during near and distant epochs of personal history.

"To cast out the enemy within by invoking the sacred fire is a necessary process. When this is done, transmutation takes place and the energies that have been imprisoned in matrices of imperfect thought and feeling are released.

"Immediately after having been dislodged from the electronic belt and purified by the flame of God, these energies ascend to the Causal Body of man, which is the repository of all good that has ever been externalized by the individual.

"Just as the electronic belt bears the records of human infamy, so the Causal Body bears witness to all true creativity. The Causal Body, then, is of the spiritual order and universe and the electronic belt is of the natural order and universe." [11]

We remember the words of First Corinthians, "There are also celestial bodies, and bodies terrestrial; but the glory of the celestial body is one, and the glory of the terrestrial is another." [12]

Again, in Lanto's discussion of energy, he tells us: "Energy fields are magnificent when they are properly qualified, for they not only surround the creator of the energy field with his own vibration of bliss, but according to the law of attraction they also magnetize the vibration of happiness and joy from many parts of the world.

"We acknowledge that the reverse is also true, and seldom do people take into account the fact that from time to time they are surrounded with negative entities—entities of fear, of doubt and of grief, which seek to invade the aura, because by their own attitudes individuals create the climate that attracts these outsiders." [13]

Let us now turn to an understanding of how to clear our misuses of energy, for in order to escape the foe without, we must conquer the foe within.

Purification of the Subconscious

Serapis has told us in the *Dossier on the Ascension:* "I am urging upon you, then, the recognition of the need to purify your memory body of all the sordid details which are stored there.

"Rid yourselves of all patterns whatsoever that are of negation, of all activities that are distinctly anti-Christ that may lie as obsession within the soul. Cleanse yourselves of all beneath the surface of consciousness that is not the purity of the Christ mediatorship of your Higher Mental Body, or Holy Christ Self." [14]

We must remember that in order to ascend, we must abandon the past to God. We cannot continue to revolve the same old hurts over and over again. Sometimes we think that we must have done something awful in the past, even if we don't know what it was. And so we start the whole spiral of self-condemnation all over again.

We need to throw it all into the violet flame and say, "Well, that's the way it was yesterday, a month ago or ten years ago. It's not going to be that way in the future, by God's grace!"

Lanto has told us that we can purify and transmute these subconscious records without having them surface in the conscious mind. The subconscious and unconscious mind has been likened to a huge iceberg and our conscious mind, the only part that we are aware of, is just the tip of this great iceberg.

The Ego and the Carnal Mind

Meru has indicated that he would like to introduce the topic of the ego. He now tells us:

"The ego is the seat of all man's problems. (The ego was also the problem behind Lucifer's fall. He fell on the line of pride.) What are known as inferiority or superiority complexes revolve entirely around the pride and frustration of the ego. But although people know these things, they continue to allow themselves to be victimized by the internal obstructions that they have created.

"The only way out is through the door of Reality. This is the escape hatch that has been provided so that the body of destructivity created by man's own negativity can be transmuted and overcome.

"As long as men remain involved in the ego, no matter what religious study they undertake, no matter what devotion they temporarily manifest, no matter how many good works they do, no matter what level of striving they attain, they will never be free from the illusion of the self that pursues them as a wanton ghost of struggling identity.

"Let all see and know for all eternity that the not-self, the shadowed-self, the personality self, is and always has been the snare of the ego and that the man or woman who lives in that consciousness must die in it. There is no possibility for such flesh and blood to inherit eternal life."[15]

Serapis adds his words of wisdom on the topic of the ego: "We watch, then, for those who do not allow the ego to be carried away in being offended or disturbed by any word, any accusation or any injustice whatever. Remember my words well, for we come to tell you of those points of the law that are found wanting and that must be met if you indeed are to accelerate on the path."

Don't React to Others

If you wear your heart on your sleeve, if you are constantly getting your feelings hurt, you have an ego problem and you had better start solving it. You cannot take your pride into the ascension flame. And if you are constantly saying that so-and-so has a big ego, examine your own ego to be sure that you are not seeing your own reflection in another.

People try so hard to perfect the human self. It will never work. Replace the human completely by the Divine, because you can never perfect the human self.

The need to call attention to oneself seems so important. We know that a naughty child gets more of his mother's attention than a good one. And so, to our detriment, we form a lifelong habit of trying to get attention.

Paul said, "I die daily."[16] Man should die daily to the finite, egoistic self. Man must also live daily to the glory of his eternal Self. We have often heard, "Man cannot see God and live." The rest of that sentence is "and live as man." When you see God, your Divine Presence, you are transformed.

If we are to progress on the path, we must learn how to avoid over reacting to others and to our own stored memories coming up from our electronic belt. For Serapis tells us, "What you object to in others may well be the polarization of your own worst fault."

It's almost as though life were a mirror—mirroring to us the faults in others that also lie buried inside of us. We may not consciously recognize that they are our faults, as they may look slightly different in another person, but the reason we object so strenuously to this person is that at some level we recognize that we are seeing the polarization of our own faults. And we don't like it!

Remember we said that devotees who come to Luxor are assigned in groups of five or more to carry out projects with other initiates whose karmic patterns lend themselves to the *maximum* friction between the lifestreams? Each group must serve together until they become harmonious, learning that those traits of character that are most offensive in others are the polarity of their own faults, and what one criticizes in another is likely to be the root of one's own misery.

We can be sure that we have also been placed in similar situations in our lives today with people who provide the greatest karmic challenge. Perhaps this explains our disagreements with our spouse, our father or mother, sisters or brothers or business associates.

Life affords us many excellent opportunities to overcome situations where individuals or conditions are not to our liking, for we cannot simply get up and walk away. We must stand, face and conquer our own returning karma by not reacting to others, even as we refuse to be dominated any longer by our own negative energy.

If we allow it, our own self-justification can also become a pitfall.

Self-Justification and Self-Defense

We know now that we have a cosmic bookkeeper in heaven who knows when we've done something right or wrong. We don't need acclaim from the world of men. Often, if we are suffering from an inferiority complex or a lack of self-esteem, we feel that it is important to excuse or justify all our actions because otherwise people would condemn or misunderstand us.

Kuthumi would like to tell us about an initiation he used to give his Franciscan brothers when he was Saint Francis. He was concerned that the brothers were spending too much energy in self-defense—defending themselves against those who had little respect for their way of life. He wanted them to concentrate on helping others who were in need. He said to them:

"And so you see, the coiled spring that men have created around the ego is actually a vain and terrible thing. And if men would, they could release it today. Remember that you have defense mechanisms. Remember that they are all stored up within you and that they seek to protect you.

"Will you give me these coiled springs of energy that I may give them to God? Then understand that in the giving of them to me, you must never again touch them. If you do, it is possible that the energy of the coiled springs of all in this group could return to you individually. Now you must let God be your defense.

"I do not mean by that that you will be unprotected, or that you will have no defense. I mean that you will have a different protection—a protection of invincible reality. You must trust in God for your defense.

"And if you should stand, as Thomas More did before the tribunal, your strength will be as the strength of ten because your heart is pure and wishes harm to no man.

"If, in this understanding, you should give your defenses to me, I shall take them from all those who give them and offer them unto the Universal and pray unto God that his light will terminate that energy of self-protection.

"Do you know that this is the way of the Christ that Christendom has failed all these years? A few of our brothers were able to externalize it and keep that vow within themselves and they never told anyone. Thus it has been kept secret until now as I choose to reveal it to you today."

Moods

We touched on moods earlier, but Lanto suggests that we need to return to this topic. He says:

"The swing of human moods is a predominant force by which the happiness and hopes of men are temporarily dashed upon the rocks. Therefore, to understand and to control the moods that seize the consciousness is to understand and master the self in a most effective way.

"First, let us show that the word *mood* is related to the word *moon*. The lunar force that acts upon the tides also affects the feeling body of man and woman and temporarily distorts their emotional nature. One of the problems involved in lunar influences is the tendency of people to identify with their moods.

"The student of the light must come apart from the world of moods. He must learn that by attuning his consciousness with the divine nature he can reverse the tide of his human moods and become the master rather than the slave of his own feelings.

"People who identify with their moods plunge headlong into a subjective sense of their problem and lose all perspective in matters in which they are emotionally involved. We therefore advocate the cultivation of a deliberate sense of detachment from the self, especially during those crucial periods when one must ask oneself the question, 'What is acting in my world?'

"When you can recognize any problem for what it is as though it were happening to someone else, you will find that it will have less hold upon you and you will be able to rise above the downward pull of mood moments.

"In the matter of moods, then, we would suggest to every student who pursues God's happiness that whenever he is invaded by a feeling that is less than God-happiness he look for the cause in his own subconscious mind and in the centering of his attention around negative ideas that he may have allowed to enter his world." [17]

Lanto wants us to understand that certain records may be

coming up on this particular day for a specific reason. We may be meant to transmute records from a certain lifetime which, in divine mercy, we know nothing about. We've been cautioned by the masters not to try to pry into our past lives. It's enough to transmute them impersonally through the violet flame.

When these negative feelings come upon you, that's the time to go out, look up at the clouds and say, "O God, you are so magnificent! Father, I thank thee!" Turning to things of a devotional nature will completely change your whole consciousness on the instant. Never let that bird that has landed on your head make a nest in your hair.

Remember the Great Divine Director's teaching that all the negativity you may be feeling may not be your own karma. It may be the floating grids and forcefields of the mass consciousness impinging on your aura. This, as well as the lunar influences at the moment, can cause you to fall into a pattern of negativity.

Lanto concludes: "All too frequently even students of the light think they can indulge themselves in moods or states of reverie simply because this is a habit they have learned to enjoy. Actually, this is a most dangerous indulgence, for the entertainment of moods can be confused with the creation of a spiritually receptive consciousness. Furthermore, prolonged involvement of the psyche in mood-energies greatly diminishes one's faculties of Christly discrimination."[18]

Lanto is pointing out that students can all too easily be drawn into the astral plane through psychedelic drugs or through curiosity about the psychic realm. It can take several embodiments for the student to heal himself of these tears in his aura caused by descending into the astral plane.

Removal of Tension

Kuthumi would like to teach the class on the subject of tension. He wants us to learn ways to overcome the stressful conditions of modern life and not let them manifest as tension. He reminds us of Jesus' admonition "Be ye in the world but not of it," for we must learn to live in a world of stress and still live successful, fulfilling lives. He begins:

"Unnecessary tension between individuals creates a sinking feeling in the belly because all discord sets up an interference with the pattern of light energy which flows through the solar plexus. The removal of tension from one's consciousness is the first step toward wholesome integration with the Divine Presence.

"The fact that you have had problems with individuals does not mean that these problems should continue. Experience should teach the soul how to relax and find freedom from oppressive states of consciousness.

"Those who serve mankind in the fields of medicine and chiropractic therapy, especially those who work with nerves, understand that when muscle groups are in a state of tension there is an enormous tie-up of energy that keeps the entire body tense. They know that the release of tension in the muscles of the body provides more energy for both mind and body.

"Likewise, those who have an understanding of the human mind know that when the psyche is tied up emotionally with diverse problems, this can cause a split personality.

"Increased mental and emotional tensions create a buildup of attracting and repelling forces that divide the self. Those who treat the mind or emotional nature of man know full well that where there is a drop in energy levels, where fatigue occurs, there is a much greater tendency to mental disorders.

"What man must do, then, is learn how to release himself from tensions—physically, mentally and emotionally. He must learn to use all of the energy that God has given him, some of which is in a state of rest and some of which is in a state of movement.

"He must learn to undo the misqualifications of energy for which he bears responsibility. He must learn to requalify that which has been misqualified. This will give him a greater quotient of energy that can be used in the development of true soul consciousness. The purpose of life is that man might master the universe through first mastering himself."[19]

A student raises his hand and says, "That sounds like excellent teaching and I am sure we all agree with it. But how do we relieve tension when we are all tied up in knots?"

Kuthumi reminds us that we need to have short mantras at hand, ready to use immediately when we feel the tension begin to build up. For example, we can say "Peace be still and know that I AM God." Go for a walk. Sing a happy song. Believe that God has a solution. Ask him to help you.

How to Handle Tension and Live Unselfishly

To conquer tension requires an act of will. If your will, your blue plume, has become inactive or weakened through drug abuse, call to Jesus, Mother Mary and the healing angels to mend and heal your chakras. These angels will, if you call to them, perform an action on your finer bodies comparable to repairing your chakras by mending them with fine threads of light. Then you must "go and sin no more,"[20] for continual use of drugs will open those chakras again.

You may be tense because you are not getting enough sleep at night and allowing your soul to ascend to the realms of light and attend the ascended masters' schools of learning there.

Proper diet, exercise, occasional short periods of fasting, can all help you build a strong body that can withstand the storms of modern life. Finally, stay harmonious, for the more you can school yourself to remain harmonious and happy, the sooner you will find tension disappearing from your life.

Selfishness

Selfishness is another of our major initiations along the path to the ascension, and a pitfall into which we can fall very easily. Selfishness is something we think we know about, but it can often come in guises we don't recognize

Elizabeth Clare Prophet has said that a sense of struggle, a lack of surrender, a susceptibility to moods, anxiety, tension and other vibrations that contaminate the aura, even extreme fatigue and exhaustion, can be caused by selfishness.

Whenever we indulge ourselves, play the martyr or accept loneliness as our lot in life, we are being selfish. If we are to be a useful chalice for God's work, we must be peaceful and happy, allowing proper time for relaxation and entertainment.

Not taking care of ourselves can be a form of selfishness. Some people say that they will work until they drop. And they have! That is not the answer. We are responsible for caring for our bodies. Billions of souls not in embodiment at present would give their all to have a body as we do.

Instead of trying to be a martyr and work unceasingly, we need proper rest every night—six, seven, eight hours or more, whatever *our* body requires, not anothers. If we allow proper time for relaxation and entertainment, we will find ourselves to be a much better chalice for the masters than when we are constantly on the edge of exhaustion, for that can be a form of selfishness also.

If we give ourselves in service, we may be tired but we will fall into bed at night and fall asleep immediately instead of worrying about whether we will be able to sleep. Not only will we find joy but we will also find a way out of many of our problems, including insomnia.

We have already discussed how some parents try to control the lives of their adult children. Often unknown to them threads of selfishness motivate people to seek unwanted and unrighteous control over the lives of others.

Inordinate grief can also be another form of selfishness. A normal grieving period following the loss of a loved one is not only expected, it is recommended for our mental and emotional health. However, inordinate, prolonged grieving is another matter entirely.

Some people grieve for years and years over the departure of a loved one. If they do so, they are actually binding the departed one to the earth. By releasing that one to go on, they are freeing them.

If we believe in life after death and in the immortality of the soul, we cannot but realize that too much grief is selfish and that by continuing in it we are holding on to the departed one and to the past. In fact, that portion of our life is now past.

We must accept that a period of our life is over—a door is closed. Often God will close one door before he opens another. Therefore we must release this one, bless him and send him on his way to higher service or to prepare for his next embodiment. He may need either a period of rest following transition or further study with the masters in their etheric retreats.

The most loving thing we can do for those who have passed on is to make calls to the angels to escort their souls to temples of light. Then we must go ahead with the balance of our service here on earth. That is the normal progression of life and if we delay it, we delay not only another soul's progress but ours also.

We have Jesus' promise to comfort us: "Let not your heart be troubled: ye believe in God, believe also in me. In my father's house are many mansions: if it were not so, I would have told you. I go to prepare a place for you. And if I go and prepare a place for you, I will come again and receive you unto myself; that where I am, there ye may be also. And whither I go, ye know and the way ye know."[21]

Loneliness can also be a manifestation of selfishness. Rather than remaining alone, you can give of yourself and your talents to others who may also be lonely. And suddenly you will find that you are happy again. If you don't know where to begin, consider the many charitable organizations that are just begging for your help. You can do hospice work, be a Big Brother or Big Sister to a child from a broken home, visit convalescent homes or read to shut-ins.

We can help others who need love in many ways. If we open our hearts to the needs of others, we will soon find that we are so busy that we have no time to feel miserable.

Anxiety

Anxiety is a state we get into when we worry over situations we can do nothing about. We can also become anxious if we fret over a situation instead of doing something about it! Anxiety seems to be one of the most difficult things to overcome. People who say that they have such great anxiety that they can scarcely function should stop and ask themselves, "What am I worrying about? What am I afraid of? Don't I trust God?"

Anxiety is a lack of faith. If you sincerely trust God, if you've given your life to him and know that he will care for you, then there is absolutely nothing to worry over or be anxious about.

Saint Germain tells us that "anxiety is the greatest deterrent to precipitation." It stops good things happening. Anxiety creates a spiral that goes on and on—the more we worry, the more problems we create.

Let go. Just release the whole situation into God's hands, knowing that at the proper time he will take care of it. One of the best ways to get control of your mind and stop worrying is to recite the Twenty-third Psalm: "The LORD is my shepherd, I shall not want." Memorize it. Say it over and over and over again until you truly believe the words of this great psalm as David himself believed them.

Psalm 23

The LORD is my shepherd; I shall not want.

He maketh me to lie down in green pastures: He leadeth me beside the still waters.

He restoreth my soul: he leadeth me in the paths of right-eousness for his name's sake.

Yea, though I walk through the valley of the shadow of death, I will fear no evil: for thou art with me; thy rod and thy staff they comfort me.

Thou preparest a table before me in the presence of mine ene-mies: thou anointest my head with oil; my cup runneth over.

Surely goodness and mercy shall follow me all the days of my life: and I will dwell in the house of the Lord forever.

When you think of all the unnecessary things you worry about in your life that dissipate your energy, remember, don't worry about what you can't change! If you are in the midst of a traffic jam and you're late for a dentist appointment, there's nothing you can do about it. Relax, turn to some music on the radio, give a few violet-flame decrees and ask God to take control of the situation. Only if you can change it, do you need to be responsible for the situation.

Saint Germain Joins the Class

At this point, Saint Germain enters the room, saying that he wants to tell us about a form of divine alchemy that can solve our problem of anxiety. He says:

"Strange as it may seem, most negative manifestations stem from anxiety. Anxiety is the great warp of life. It warps perspective without producing any perceptible benefit whatsoever.

"Anxiety is the cause of people's tendency to hoard the goods of this world. Like frantic squirrels they pile up their winter's supply of nuts. They accumulate an oversupply of every imaginable item, and they deprive themselves of happiness by their unwarranted concerns and their unnecessary and time-consuming preparations for every eventuality.

"Anxiety is a symptom of insecurity. It stems from a man's incorrect concept of himself and from his lack of perspective. Many people feel unfulfilled, unloved, unwanted, or they are not sure of just what they should be doing with their lives.

"Their uncertainties under adverse conditions are easily turned into mental and emotional states of depression bordering on extreme self-deprecation. The hard experiences that have come to many in childhood and in later years, creating stress and strains and producing the fruit of bitterness, have *prevented their development of that refined spirit which would enable them to shed their anxieties.*

"I urge you to make your God-determination that you are going to clean your consciousness inside out. Anxiety must go! It must be replaced by faith and solemn confidence in the outworking of the divine plan.

"You were born to win, and I say this to counter the lie that man was 'born to lose.' And if you will make the statement 'I AM born to win!' as an act of supreme faith, it will overcome the will to fail—a deadly weight of sin if there ever was one.

"You must realize that anxieties must go and make a conscious determination that it shall be done. You can make it if you try—TRY!" [22]

The Will to Fail

The fact that we might need to conquer the will to fail may come as a surprise to us.

Are you in the habit of saying to yourself, "I never can do anything right anyway, so why try," or "there's no use in trying to do that because I'm too old, too young, too uneducated, too something."? If you think this way, you may have the will to fail. And if you continue making excuses to yourself, someday you'll find that you *have* failed. Your negative thoughts will have caused it to happen.

Every victory is a victory of love, and the absence of love is the definition of every failure. We are never given a test for which we have not been prepared. Our preparation resides in our heart flame—our threefold flame in the secret chamber of our heart.

When a student is presented with a test, often he will mix the ingredients of his subconscious—his human questioning, doubts, fears, intellect, academic training—and substitute all these in place of leading with his heart and his threefold flame. And so he can fail minor tests or major tests or sometimes completely desert the Path.

When we look at the world and the people in the world, we can understand why we fail. We are taught to lead with our intellect, with our emotions, with our subconscious and unconscious—all these things are the gods of the human mind. And so we approach a problem with only these ingredients.

They are never adequate to the test, and people again and again fail initiations on the Path where they substitute worldly success and the development of the ego for love—love of God or love of an ideal.

One factor that can cause a person to will to fail is fear—fear of failure, fear of trying because we may fail. If we are one who feels tormented by fear, remember that "perfect love casteth out fear."[23] We should sit down and decide what it is that we're afraid of. What terrible thing is going to happen? We may even have a hard time putting it on paper, but if we can, then we should write it down, burn it in a petition to the Karmic Board and forget about it. Accept that God's love can enter into your heart and replace your fear and your will to fail.

Become As a Little Child

Kuthumi suggests that the best way to overcome all this is to take to heart Jesus' words, "Whosoever shall not receive the kingdom of God as a little child, he shall not enter therein."[24] To manifest the little-child consciousness is to develop the masterful Christ consciousness that will successfully take dominion over the earth.

And as this is a topic close to Serapis' heart. He takes up the theme: "So simple and childlike are the attributes of the kingdom that men overlook them and thus they pass them by. The blessings of God are all around life everywhere. Life is complete with the most wonderful shadings of bliss which could be enjoyed by the Godhead himself. Yet in men the power of perception, the sensitivity to perceive life itself, seems to be lacking.

"'Having eyes to see, they see not; having ears to hear, they hear not.'[25] Neither do they sense nor touch the reality of

God. One of the greatest blessings that can ever come to an embodied individual is the reawakening of the divine sense and childlike wonder which so many had in manifestation very early in their lives.[26]

"The first step is to become as a little child. You must become the child of innocence before you can mature to be the Christed man or Christed woman. When you are a tiny babe, total trust and faith and hope and charity are yours. You have not burdened your heart, you have not burdened yourself to become a cynic in the world. You are calm and serene, with the absolute conviction that your life is in God, that God is caring for you.

"The most essential quality of becoming this tiny babe is to understand the quality of helplessness. When you are totally helpless, then you must allow God to work his work within you. You can truly say as the child of Christ, 'I can of mine own self do nothing; but the Father that dwelleth in me, he doeth the works.'[27] You are at peace and life is yours to conquer because you are God in manifestation.

"Now you are ready for the disciplines whereby the babe will become the child. Now your habitation is a cosmos, a world filled with light and yet with shadows and darkness. The little child in innocence begins to learn the ways of the world—a little fall, tears and demands that cannot be fulfilled—and therefore you learn to fulfill your own demands.

"If you retain the innocence of the little child, you will become the little child who leads all aspects of the creation into the knowledge of the Christ. The little child is the leader of the Aquarian age. You must not only become the little child, but you must remain the little child. Better to be hurt again and again than to have the cynicism of the existentialists."

As El Morya has said, "The result of becoming as a little child is rebirth, being 'born again' into the consciousness of the kingdom of heaven."

A Little Child
by Jesus the Christ

A little child shall lead them—
The eye so meek and mild
A little child shall feed them—
Where is the little child?

Right within you, golden man!
His flaming image flashes
Expanding now as son of man
Meteoric flashes!

The way ye know, the way to go
Reveals in sudden flashes
That to live you must forgive
Man for sodden clashes!

Victory's gleam will send a stream
Renewing each man's portion
The dead shall rise unto the skies
And live in purest thought!

This life is real and will not steal
The truth that I have brought—
My Word abiding now is hiding
In the soul that God hath wrought.

This little child
So meek and mild
Is man whom God hath taught!

∵ *If you wish to further enhance your study before proceeding to Chapter 17, you will find exercises on p. 232.*

🜂

CHAPTER SEVENTEEN

Love: The Initiation of Aquarius

As Serapis Bey takes his place at the lectern to begin this evening's instruction he says, "I must explain something to you before I begin my lecture on love. Some of you may have a rather unrealistic idea of the true meaning of the word love.

"The contemplation of this subject can often bring to mind pictures of bliss and unending pleasure. And this can be true if it is divine love upon which you are meditating. But so often students are apt to dream about a sticky, mushy sensation of love that includes a sense of selfishness and is interested only in the fulfillment of personal desires.

"True love is a divine quality that may even be severe at times in its demands on the initiate. In order to experience divine love, you must broaden your horizon to include the needs of the world and those of your fellowman.

"There are so many substitutes for love upon earth that one can scarcely find a single petal of purest love among a thousand folk taken at random here or there! Men are so wont to accept a substitute for purest love.

"Tonight I shall be addressing two tests of love which you may never have considered: the one, giving intense love to others without expecting recognition or thanks; and the second, asking God to intensify his love upon you as the chastening. Have you ever considered that chastening is love, even though it may be rather uncomfortable?

"I urge you to keep an open mind during tonight's lecture and then meditate on the subject of true, divine love, the love of God, the masters, angels and elementals. For the next *several weeks as you go to sleep at night, call for the Electronic Presence of the masters who serve on the love ray to overshadow you and teach you what love really is.*

"And now, we will begin."

The Path of Love

Serapis continues: "The path of the ascension is the path of love. It is love and the dream of love fulfilled. The disciplines for the initiations of the ascension into higher consciousness can only be borne by love, by the heart and the soul so filled with love for God, the Great Guru, that it will endure unto the end of the cycles of human consciousness.

"The path is straight and narrow, as you have heard. The climb is over rigid heights, scaling jagged cliffs, over precipice and abyss into the high road, into the mountains of the Himalayas. Souls are called and impelled by love, the love of the mountaineers, the love of the Elohim who have anchored their focuses in the heights of the mountains of the earth.

"Love and love alone is the key to overcoming. For God is love. And where selfishness lurks there will be compromise, there will be the moment's hesitation and the battle is lost, the moment of indecision when the idling of energy creates a gap in the spiraling and the flow and the movement of God.

"Therefore in the hour of decision, in the moment when the question arises out of that human questioning to be or not to be on the path of initiation, we ask a question. For we are the hierarchs of Luxor, of the Retreat of the Ascension Flame. We guard the steely-white, intense sacred fire that can be contained only by those who live in the purity of love. And therefore, while you are engaged in your human questioning of the Guru, I ask the supreme question: How much do you love, how great is your love?

"Is your love great enough to make the sacrifice for the overcoming, for the Path, for the cause of the Great White Brotherhood that others among mankind might also receive the teachings, the law and the understanding of the fulfillment of the promise of love?

"Faced with this question, the individual must either retreat into his old ways of the self-centered existence or come forth from that cocoon of selfishness and fly with the wings of the Spirit, the wings of love that are the certain victory.

"There is a key in the disciplines to higher consciousness. The key is not to become entangled in the labyrinth of human questioning and the fears and the doubts and specters of the night that haunt that labyrinth. The key—instead of taking a thousand steps through the astral plane—is to take one step into the arms of the I AM Presence, into the plane of the Christ.

"In the moment when you would indulge your pettiness, your argumentation, your human nonsense, your dalliance in childishness, in that moment you instantly let go and you let God be the light that swallows you up in the victory of love. The love that is your victory is your own love that is God made manifest within you.

"Love God enough so that you do not need to satisfy human desire. If you can sustain your energies upon your I AM Presence and upon the light, you will receive the energy necessary to deal with all outer circumstances (karma) and that without traveling through them in your emotions, in your mental concepts, in your memory and in physical labor. Think, then, upon this.[1]

"Only love can draw forth from within your being the necessary components for your ascension. You cannot love yourself more than you love God. Without love you can only go so far on the Path and then you become brittle."[2]

Love God

Saint Germain is the master of the love flame of the Aquarian age. The perversion of that flame is hatred, so we will need to master the initiations of love and we will also need to master the initiations of the perversions of love. In Jesus' two-thousand-year cycle of the age of Pisces, we were meant to follow his example and become the Christ. Instead of doing that, many of us outpictured the opposite of his flame—fear, doubt, human questioning, records of death.

Of the several kinds of love, one is giving intense love to God in our fellowman without desiring recognition. If we have maturity of heart, we will have the courage to take this test of love. The Buddha said that the coming of age of the heart is courage —*coeur-age*. To pass this test of love, we can not expect to be patted on the back and told, "Oh, you are so wonderful. Everyone is so grateful for all the things you do for them."

This gushy kind of love often contains a hidden motive— a motive for recognition, a motive to gain friends, a motive to possess and manipulate. If we believe that loving behavior should be acknowledged by all kinds of attentions and adorn-ments, we can get our outer mind to speak flattery to us because we enjoy the flattery. So let's see if we have the courage to love silently and quietly without craving the return that we constantly expect from love.

Thus the first initiation of love under Serapis is giving intense love to God in our fellowman, to the soul of our fellowman, without desiring recognition or thanks. Think of the love of the angels and the elementals who labor twenty-four hours a day ceaselessly, and most of us don't even know they're there.

Ninety percent of the people on earth don't know that angels and elementals exist because they can't see them. And yet they labor on and on with absolutely no reward from mankind. That is true Love with a capital *L*.

The Chastening

The second initiation of love under Serapis is to ask God to intensify his love upon us to chasten us. Chastening is difficult for many to endure, so if you ask for this initiation, get ready! It may come through a friend. It may come through an outburst from someone. It may come through a difficult situation, but it will come.

The masters tell us that the discipline, or judgment, of God is an action of love. God loves us so much that he lets our karma fall so we will realize where we have erred and return to him. Thus we can quickly correct our error, put it into the flame and move on.

We may call it mercy to have karma set aside, and mercy it is because it allows us to grow. But there is a higher mercy that is justice. It is also judgment. We read in Hebrews, "Whom the Lord loveth he chasteneth, and scourgeth every son whom he receiveth."[3]

Serapis says: "To embark on the path toward mastery, achievement, victory and the ascension is an initiatic process. The few in ages past have walked through the gates whose narrow markings may not be too comfortable to those over-stuffed with the vanities of the world."[4]

Many of us can't seem to understand why our neighbors and friends lead such a charmed life and have so few problems, while for us, no matter how hard we try, occasionally things go wrong. We realize that we have asked for the chastening love of God that will speed us on our path.

Serapis speaks of that love: "If you would be truth, if you would convey the truth, if you would convey the flow of light, of healing from the Presence, as Above, so below, remember that you are the tree that must be pruned and that the chastening of the law is the action of God's love. You ought to look with utter compassion upon those parts of life who have no one to chasten them.

"I say to you, if you are chastened, know that you are loved. And if you would be free of the chastening, then I say, be free of the love as well as the chastening. For the two go hand in hand.

"And when you feel the absence of the disciplines of the law, it is time to feel the air and to say, 'Where did love go? Out the window, I know.' And so you can't have one without the other. And if you would be love to mankind, I say, be love in the fullness of purity."

Therefore, to restate the two tests of love: the first is to give intense love to the God in your fellowman without desiring recognition or thanks; and the second is to ask God to intensify his love upon you and chasten you.

∼ *If you wish to further enhance your study before proceeding to Chapter 18, you will find exercises on p. 234.*

CHAPTER EIGHTEEN

❦

Surrender to the Will of God

We begin our class this night with some teaching from Serapis on how to surrender to the will of God. He says, "Surrender is one of the most misunderstood initiations on the path to the ascension. Millions of souls truly want to surrender their will to the will of God but they don't know how. They don't know where to begin.

"Sweet surrender to the Presence of God is initiated, first of all, in the will. The will is the key whereby the human self has its say. You have willed lesser images. You have willed imperfections. You have willed subservience to others and to the world order. You have closed your eyes to the truth of God that stands glaringly apparent even to a child.[1]

"The aspect of 'will' is vital to our freedom in the ascension. A certain part can be accomplished by decrees and by the violet flame, but the will, the conscious will, must be an integral part of the process. For the ascension is a do-it-yourself project. I can point out ways to you. I can give you the keys that have helped many, but unless you take them and make them a part of your life, we're both wasting our time.

"Listen carefully, beloved ones, and take complete notes, because I will require from you a paper that states just what the will of God means to you. I will ask you to suggest how you plan to make your human will one with the will of God. But first, remember what Kuthumi has told us:

"'Surrender to God is not death. It is life. It is beauty. It is hope. It is the wings of the mind borne upward into the airiness and lightness of celestial realities. No empty void is there, but the natives of cosmos in all of their blazing reality—

ministering spirits, angels, cosmic beings, cosmic masters—
one and all, as the higher kin of every man, hold their offer-
ings of eternal sweetness for the purification and release of the
souls of men from bondage.' [2]

"*Since El Morya is the Lord of the First Ray of the Will*
of God," Serapis continues, *"I will be giving you some quotes*
from his devotional book, The Sacred Adventure. *Morya's*
writings are perhaps the best way to help you differentiate
between your human will and the will of God."

The Sacred Adventure

El Morya writes:

"Down through the centuries men have discussed the will of
God as though it were a thing apart from the will of man, bearing no resemblance to an offering that affords the best gifts to
man. Contrary to human opinion, the will of God seeks to vest
man with his immortal birthright and never to deprive him of
his freedom.

" 'The will of God is good.' The affirmation of this childlike
statement over and over again is a means whereby the mind can
be stilled and the mounting crescendo of human emotions dimin-
ished. In this way your conscious mind is insisting that your
subconscious and unconscious come under the control of your
God mind, your superconscious mind.

" 'How can I know the will of God?' This is the cry of millions. Man presupposes that the divine will is hiding from him,
as though it were a part of the Eternal God to play hide-and-seek
with him.

"Not so! The will of God is inherent within life and merely
awaits the signal of release from man's will in order to ray forth
the power of dominion to the world of the individual.

"There is a sovereign link between the mortal will and the
Immortal. In the statement of Jesus 'It is the Father's good pleasure to give you the kingdom,'[3] men can be aware of the eternal
will as the fullest measure of divine love.

"Release, then, your feelings of possessiveness over your own life. Surrender the mean sense of sin and rebellion, the pitiful will to the self-privilege which engenders bondage.

"See the will of God as omnipresent and complete, the holy beat of the sacred heart throbbing within your own. Know and understand that surrender is not oblivion but a point of beginning and of greater joy."[4]

The Will of God Is Good

The Brotherhood has told us that we will hear intoned in all the retreats the mantra "Not my will, not my will, not my will but thine be done." We can even make it echo to the rhythm of our steps as we walk down the street. We may let the mantra just flow through our mind, thousands of times a day, flooding our subconscious and unconscious mind. Know that thousands of ascended masters are also repeating this mantra with us.

El Morya personifies the will of God, for he has become one with that will. If you sincerely want to know how to become one with it also, call to El Morya when you go to bed at night, ask him to place his Electronic Presence over you as you sleep. Say, "Beloved El Morya, I want to know God's will. I want to know how to surrender."

You may think you have consciously surrendered, but the hidden part of the iceberg is formed by your subconscious and unconscious will. That is what Morya needs to work with, and he can tell you how to get control of the iceberg of your subconscious and unconscious mind.

Abraham Was a Friend of God

Another way to surrender to the will of God is just to ask God to take command of your life. Talk to him, saying, "Father, I surrender my will to you."

Mark Prophet used to say often, "And God did not impute sin to Abraham, because Abraham was a 'Friend of God.'"[5] One goal we might have in this lifetime is to become a friend of God as Abraham was so that our sins will not be a burden to us. Abraham understood how to let God's will work through him because he knew that all the power that flowed through him was the power of God. And he surrendered everything to God's will, even his favorite son.

Jesus, you remember, said, "The words that I speak unto you I speak not of myself: but the Father that dwelleth within me, he doeth the works."[6]

To hold back the smallest particle of one's individuality as a personal possession is forbidden in the ascension retreat. Total surrender is the order of the day. Serapis knows that we become the ascension flame by the trial by fire, by surrender.

One warning however, we may think we have truly surrendered, but it is not a one-time thing. Although we make up our mind today, another problem arises tomorrow or the same problem takes a different face.

Paul said, "I die daily."[7] That is exactly what it takes. We don't pass a test just once, God tests us again and again. Remember, it's not a one-time surrender. Every day and every hour, we can submit into the fire of the will of God our desires, our dreams, our plans. If they do not turn out to be God's will, allow them to be consumed the flame.

Let the flame transmute all that is not the will of God. Then let God give the transmuted energy back to us. Examine it and see the diamonds of the will of God that we have been given.

Let us return to the wisdom of *The Sacred Adventure*. El Morya says: "God sought to bestow, and the best gift that he could give was the gift of his will. For by his will he framed the far-off worlds, and by his will he sustained the momentum of life within each cell.

"The will of God is a security beyond belief, beyond faith and even beyond manifestation, for it is the solemnly beautiful beaming of the tenderness of the Father's care for his children.

"It is the strength of the right arm of the Almighty. It is the fire of his devotion and the best gift to his children. There is safety in it and the strength that fashions security for the ages and beyond."[8]

The Sense of Struggle

Each one of us individually must put an end to the sense of struggle in our world. No one else can do it for us. It takes an act of will every time a struggle arises. Remember, Saint Germain has said that "it is the sense of struggle that makes the struggle." Yet don't let your mind idle in neutral either. Make a decision one way or another.

This also requires an act of will, for it is much easier to just sit back and let matters take their course. When you pray, "Not my will but thine be done, O God," you will gradually become the will of God in expression everywhere. A change takes place within you, for you no longer suffer the pains of countering the will of God with your own human will. Over time your sense of struggle ceases, for your human will has become the will of God and the resistance between the two has dissolved. Then the struggle is over.

El Morya has pointed out that "it is absolutely true that the will of God does not struggle. It does not struggle with the will of men. On the contrary, it is the will of man that struggles with the will of God. The will of God is quick—it moves, it is rest in motion, it is the action of a cosmos."

The reason we must surrender our human will is that it keeps us from becoming immortal, God-free beings because of the very nature of its frequency, its vibration. Remember, the difference between the ascended and the human octaves is in the vibratory rate. We are too slow and too dense down here.

We will find that the Divine Will is what we always wanted anyway. We simply never understood what it was. It's the Real Self, who we are and what we are. For in actuality, the will of God is our design, our blueprint, the law that governs the movement of the fluid in our cells.

"Above all," says El Morya in closing his explanation of the will of God, "understand always that, complex and all-embracing though it may be, the will of God can always be reduced to the common denominator of love, life and light."[9]

Rebellion

Many sincere souls are still struggling with the problem of rebellion against God. We can become so tied up in knots over rebellion and so busy analyzing and fighting this rebellion that we become exhausted.

The answer is to forget even the consciousness of rebellion. Simply immerse yourself in El Morya—read his book, listen to his dictations, give his decrees, talk to him, love him. Say to him, "I am turning over to you all of my human consciousness and I am accepting your God consciousness in exchange. Please help me to transmute my lesser self."

When you get to the place where you're so in love with God, you're so in love with the will of God and all its virtues and all its wonders and the power of the mastery and the freedom that it gives you, lo and behold, your rebellion doesn't exist anymore! It has been dissolved by the intense exchange of love that you have had with the master.

An important way to tackle the human consciousness is to ignore it and to dive into the sea of God. When you come up again, you will find that you have an entirely new perspective. What looked like a mountain has become a grain of sand.

Before we leave this subject, we should be sure we understand what we are surrendering. We are surrendering our human will, our human ego and our human intellect to the Divine Will of God, to our Higher Self, to our Christ Mind. We are replacing our human self as, little by little, we put on our Divine Self. Just ask God. He will help you.

A Novena to the Great Divine Director

Saint Germain has given us another method of finding the will of God in our life. He suggests we give a novena, a nine day prayer, to the Great Divine Director for guidance in our affairs.

The Great Divine Director is a being of great attainment who works closely with Saint Germain to bring in the new age of Aquarius. He directs great beams of light from his heart that have crystallized into dazzling jewels of light. He wears these jewels in a belt around his waist that reaches to below his knees. His mantra refers to this blue belt.

The Great Divine Director has told us that he holds within his consciousness the scroll of the divine plan for every living soul on earth and beyond. He asks us to call for the soul to remember her divine plan and to bring it into outer manifestation. If our call is in accordance with the will of God, angels of the Great Divine Director will go forth to help us.

Begin the novena by placing yourself somewhere where you will not be disturbed. With a blank sheet of paper and a pen, meditate upon your divine plan by visualizing a white sphere before you. Approximately two feet in diameter, this sphere is the symbol of your own cosmic consciousness that you contact in meditation. Call to your I AM Presence, the Great Divine Director and Saint Germain to assist you in calling forth the divine plan for your life.

Light a candle and consecrate it to your opportunity to fulfill your cosmic destiny. Let the flame be the focus of the threefold flame of love, wisdom and power that burns on the altar of your heart.

Now take your pen and write on the white page before you, which symbolizes the white page God has given you as the gift of life, the goals you desire to accomplish in this life. Write down your fondest hopes, your impossible dreams, your heart's longings, your desire for soul fulfillment, your educational goals, your spiritual and material expectations, the service you desire to render unto God and man.

You many need to write and rewrite this outline of your life. When you are satisfied that your list of goals is realistic as well as idealistic, make two copies. Place one between the pages of your Bible and burn the other so that the message is conveyed by the angels to the Great Divine Director and to the Lords of Karma.

Give the mantra for divine direction fourteen times (see below). You can also give it with your left hand on the Bible, and the decree in your right hand. Repeat this for nine days (or for thirty-three days), and each day at the conclusion of your meditation and mantra, take your pen and write down on a fresh white page the thoughts and the feelings that come to you.

As you give the mantra and the meditation, you are planting the seeds of your own cosmic consciousness at conscious and subconscious levels within your being. These seeds will germinate. But do not be concerned if no immediate answer comes to your outer consciousness.

While you are waiting for the results of this sacred alchemy, be sure to continue your decrees to the violet flame to purify your four lower bodies from the residue of your personal and planetary karma. In this way, clarity of direction will appear.

Here is the mantra to the Great Divine Director. You may list in the preamble whatever you are asking direction for:

In the name of the Presence of God I AM in me and my own Christ Self, I call to the beloved Great Divine Director for divine direction in my affairs, especially for (list your concerns).

> Divine Director, come,
> Seal me in thy ray;
> Guide me to my home
> By thy love I pray.
>
> Refrain:
>   Thy blue belt protect my world,
>   They dazzling jewels so rare
>   Surround my form and adorn
>   With essence of thy prayer!

Make us one, guard each hour;
Like the sun's radiant power
Let me be, ever free
Now and for eternity.

Blessed Master R,
You are near, not far;
Flood with light, God's own might
Radiant like a star.

Divine Director dear,
Give me wisdom pure
Thy power ever near
Helps me to endure.

Shed thy light on me,
Come, make me whole;
Banner of the free,
Mold and shape my soul.

And in full faith I consciously accept this manifest, manifest, manifest right here and now with full power, eternally sustained, all powerfully active, ever expanding, and world enfolding until all are wholly ascended in the light and free! Beloved I AM, Beloved I AM, Beloved I AM!

Serapis closes his class this evening with a little devotional mantra from El Morya.

The Light of God's Will
by El Morya

The light of God's will
Flows ever through me
The flow of real purpose
I now clearly see
O pearly white radiance
Command all life free!

☙ *If you wish to further enhance your study before proceeding to Chapter 19, you will find exercises on p. 235.*

CHAPTER NINETEEN

❦

Faith, the Antidote to Doubt and Fear

I know of no one more qualified to speak on the subject of faith than Archangel Michael, our glorious Archangel of the First Ray and his beloved archeia, Faith," said Serapis. "Michael's title is Prince of the Archangels and Defender of the Faith. He has also been called the Angel of Deliverance because he has offered to free souls from their lower nature as well as from psychic energy and the astral plane if they will call to him and ask to be cut free.

"Archangel Michael is a being of great attainment, strength and love. Aeons ago he underwent the same tests that you are now taking. And because he successfully passed those tests, he can stand before you with the courage of God to defend all life.

"To assist in cutting you free, Archangel Michael has fashioned a sword of blue flame from pure light energy. He has myriad bands of angels who work twenty-four hours a day rescuing souls. They have served for thousands of years, and Michael says he will never give up until the last child of light on this planet has risen to his God Source in the ritual of the ascension.

What Is Faith?

"Faith is a natural gift of God," says Archangel Michael. "It is immortal substance. Faith is the power by which your dreams come true. Faith is the will to be and to do. Faith is the action of the sacred Word. Faith is the voice of God I heard."

Faith is also the eternal substance of the presence of light, and as Hebrews tells us, "Faith is the substance of things hoped for, the evidence of things not seen." [1]

Archangel Michael asks us: "Will you see for yourself, if only for the purpose of experimentation, what a difference faith makes? Faith may seem to be an ingredient that only children and fools rely upon. But it is not difficult even for the scientist to discover that it possesses a tangibility all of its own.

"Faith will open the inner eyes wide with wonder. It will reveal to you your inner strength. It will show you aspects of your being that you never dreamed existed, and it will show you how to contact and implement in a practical way the potential that is locked within these aspects of being.

"Faith is the bridge that the consciousness must build before it can traverse the abyss that separates the finite from the Infinite. Once crossed, the bridge is no longer necessary and the arduous journey is forgotten in the joy of discovery and the welcome of reality.

"Therefore it is essential to give faith a chance, even if at first your motive be selfish. You need to open the door. You need to build the bridge. You need to believe, even if momentarily, in order that you may become filled with grace and with the great cosmic potential of life that you really are."

Having given us his presence and the flame of his faith, Michael departs, saying that he will leave it to Serapis to continue this teaching.

Serapis turns to us and says: "Think of the best quality you know of yourself or of a friend, one you trust. Think of one quality that you know that is never-failing in that friend—the affirmation of your reality, faith, diligence.

"A quality such as this is a pattern of the ascension already set, already crystallized as a jewel, because a lifestream has outpictured that quality for century upon century. It will be the most notable point of nobility of a given soul, and that which you appreciate most."

A Doubt Born of Pride

Serapis reads from the *Dossier on the Ascension:*

"There is a doubt that is born of pride which causes individuals to shrink from anything they at first deem to be unprovable. This doubt dispels faith, throws the consciousness into a state of trepidation, elongates confusion and terminates the fruit of faith.

"No man wishes to be the victim of a hoax, and his personal pride tells him that unless he is wary he may very well be. Thus, the sophistication of earthly reason overrides the great tangible realities of Almighty God that dwell in the invisible realm and are functional in all outer manifestation." [2]

As we ponder Serapis' words we realize that we have often wondered why people accept some things without question and immediately reject the great truths of God. We know that we cannot see the wind, yet it blows and we accept that it is there.

I am constantly amazed that we walk right up to electronic doors, totally trusting that they will open. We never think that perhaps we'll bang our nose. If we can place implicit faith in an electronic device, we have to ask ourselves why we can't trust God. When we put our paycheck in an envelope and drop it in the mailbox, never questioning that it will arrive at the bank and be credited to our account, that is faith!

In most cases, the battle of life is not won on momentous decisions, it is won on the little day-to-day experiences whereby we turn our heart to God in faith and trust and receive the grace that cuts us free from the negative aspects of life that have momentarily trapped us.

Archangel Michael has told us that the pathway of faith is like a mighty shimmering ribbon of light substance connecting us with our God Presence. This visualization can help us to see ourselves connected to God and free us from feeling that we are separated from God.

To help us free ourselves, Archangel Michael has fashioned a sword of blue flame from pure light substance. We can see this as beautiful, crackling, scintillating blue light every time we call to Archangel Michael.

Doubt, Fear and Records of Death

One of the chief problems we encounter in discovering the Real Self is doubt, fear, human questioning and records of death—our Piscean initiation. Perhaps we have even heard it said that today is the tomorrow we worried about yesterday.

Some skeptics seem to feel that they must put God in a test tube in order to prove him. Their inability to trust is their greatest obstacle to faith. It's the same doubt that tells us we must pick apart a rose, petal by petal, to see what makes it so beautiful. All of a sudden the rose has gone, for we've destroyed it. Instead of accepting the beauty of the rose, we dissected it.

Michael, the Prince of Archangels, has said that we must stand fast and conquer fear as no cause for fear exists anywhere in cosmos except in ourselves. Nor does any cause for doubt exists anywhere but in ourselves. And our tendency to keep questioning God is also our own.

Michael offers us a wonderful bargain when he says, "Give me your attention. Give me your doubts, your questionings, and I will give you my faith." Why don't we accept his offer and prove him for ourselves!

Sometimes all we need to know to successfully pass a difficult test is that we have friends of light—archangels, angels, ascended masters who are upholding us and praying for our success. However, when an archangel offers us his faith, we should think twice about refusing his gift.

Michael says, "When sight is obtained, of what need is faith? It is not I who need faith—except to give it away—but it is you who require it."

Perfect Love Casts Out Fear

Think of the saying "perfect love casteth out fear because fear hath torment."[3] Perhaps we need to write this little mantra on a card and place it on our mirror or in our wallet where we can look at it often.

Saint Germain once said that we could do anything if we love enough, for love is the antithesis of fear and faith is the opposite of doubt. Serapis said that men prove the law by doing the law. They see truth by becoming truth. They ascend by faith and not by doubt.

Our doubts and fears will not allow us to stand in the ascension flame, for we would be consumed. So we have to throw away our doubts and fears, and the way to do this is to throw them into the violet flame.

Meru offers us help when he says, "The key to escape is simple. If you will remain steadfast in a childlike sense of wonder and trust in God, we can this day dispel all doubt and fear from your consciousness."[4]

Atheists, Agnostics and Skeptics

A person with a scientific bent is usually a very detailed person and often feels the need to prove things logically. But there is a logic of the head and a logic of the heart and sometimes we have to listen to our heart and trust in what God says to us.

Hilarion, the Lord of the Fifth Ray, is the master for skeptics, agnostics and atheists. He was Saul of Tarsus who became Paul after Jesus spoke to him on the road to Damascus. Because he struggled with doubt in his life as Saul, he knows that he can help us now. Jesus said, "If thou canst believe, all things are possible to him that believeth."[5]

Hilarion has made us a promise. He said that if we feel that we have to reduce everything to what we believe is scientific proof, if we can't accept anything on faith, call to him and he'll help us. If you know someone who is a skeptic, call to Hilarion and he'll be happy to help them—according to their free will of course.

Often many people are skeptics because in a past life they believed strongly in their particular faith but were disappointed after death to find that their beliefs weren't entirely true. They had not been taught about reincarnation or karma and suddenly after leaving their body, they found that they had to come back and reembody again.

Perhaps they expected to be sitting in heaven at the right hand of the Father and were so hurt on finding out the truth that they became skeptics, fearing to believe anyone or anything again. When these souls return to embodiment, they are scarred, often refusing to trust any religion.

Hilarion says that there are many, many good people in this condition. He promises to take them in his arms, and love them and train them. He says, "Give me your agnostics, your atheists, your skeptics. I will enfold them in my green ray of truth."

If any members of your family feel that religion is not for them, you might commend them to Hilarion at night. Ask in the name of their Christ Self and according to their free will that their souls be taken to his retreat over Crete and taught there while they are out of the body. Ask that they might be told the truth.

Protection

You may be having trouble ridding yourself of your doubts and fears because you need more protection and are therefore an easy target for the forces of darkness. Archangel Michael has told us: "Cling to that sword of blue flame and use it. Do you think that the hosts of light who have direct access to the consciousness of God would use a sword if it were not effective, if they did not need it? I say to you, you need the armor and you need the sword of Archangel Michael. You need the fires of protection.

"It is utter folly to arise from your bed and leave your homes at any time of the day or night to go out into the world without making invocations for assistance from my band, from my legions and from myself and the light which I carry. For, precious hearts, you live in the astral sea. You are submerged in the mass consciousness. You walk through that consciousness.

"My angels would never go forth to do battle without the armor of light and the full protection of the Law. I tell you, the tide is rising, ever rising, and mankind and the children of the light are inundated by the sewers of their own consciousness.

"To go forth and to be soiled, to be immersed in that substance is sheer folly, sheer stupidity. For you know, precious hearts, we cannot interfere with the dangers that assail you, we cannot come to arrest the spirals of danger to your person without your having first made the calls.

"Do not wait until you enter your cars or means of transportation to begin to make your calls. It is necessary that you are harmonious, for if you invoke the assistance of the legions of light and there is irritation in your world, you can be certain that the forces of darkness, who are ever alert to see when you are vulnerable, will move in.

"They will use individuals who are totally tied to the mass consciousness to do foolish things on the highways and to cause accidents of all kinds. Therefore I say, use the armor, use the power of the spoken Word, and raise the sword of blue flame.

"Where is that sword? It is in your heart. You can qualify the flame within your heart with the sword of mercy or the sword of blue flame or a scepter of authority. Thus you place your hand to your heart and you say, 'In the name of Almighty God, release the energies of blue flame into my right hand. Let me go forth with the sword of Archangel Michael to challenge the darkness and those who are aligned with darkness this day.'

"This you must do. And if you keep the energies and the spirit of Archangel Michael with you always, you will win."

Many carry a small picture of Archangel Michael in their car and say his mantra whenever they travel. Here it is again, in case you have forgotten it. Use it not only in your car but all day long. As you give these words aloud or silently, see a glorious, powerful blue archangel overshadowing you and protecting you.

> Lord Michael before, Lord Michael behind,
> Lord Michael to the right,
> Lord Michael to the left,
> Lord Michael above, Lord Michael below,
> Lord Michael, Lord Michael wherever I go.
>
> I AM his love protecting here.
> I AM his love protecting here.
> I AM his love protecting here.

Nightmares and Sleep Problems

Many people have difficulty sleeping at night and are frightened by nightmares. If we are not protected when we leave our bodies at night, we are vulnerable to attack by the forces of darkness. Archangel Michael has recommended that we invoke his full armor of protection before we go to sleep.

If you can't visualize it, try this. Step by step as you're lying in bed, imagine putting on his crystalline helmet of pure light substance, then taking up his sword, his shield, his boots, his gauntlets, until you are completely covered and invincible.

Once you are protected by Michael's armor, ask him to go with you and to place his Electronic Presence over you as you leave your body at night. Ask him to be with you throughout the night, whether you're going to a temple to study or whether you're traveling with him and his legions.

Ask him to help you reenter your body in the morning, for that is when the beings of the astral plane try to bother you—when you're half asleep and half awake, when the alarm has rung and you know you should get up and yet you want to sleep just five more minutes. That's when you are in the astral plane, not really asleep and yet not fully awake either.

The Goddess of Purity teaches that sleep should be an occasion for "recharging the vital, pure energies of your being." She says: "It ought to be a time when the batteries of human life can be literally filled with the purity of the divine Presence. It is necessary before you fall asleep to establish some pattern of upward elevation in consciousness that will lead you to find those pathways where the spirit of purity can sweep through your finer bodies while you sleep and leave you the blessedness of the childlike ascended master consciousness."

One more reason why you may not be sleeping well is because you Christ Self has awakened you as it is not safe for you to be out of your body. At certain times when the energy is bad enough, you need to get up and change the vibration in the room.

The Great Divine Director suggests that you go into the kitchen, get a glass of water, say a couple of prayers—then go back to bed. Don't just lie there where a projection is on you and try to get back to sleep.

Here, then, are the three reasons why you may not be sleeping well:

1. You need more purity
2. You need more protection
3. Your Christ Self may be saying, "I'm sorry, this is not the right time to sleep. So get up and deal with that energy and then go back to sleep."

You may need a thoughtform for the second possibility. Catholics might like to think of Saint Christopher who protected the Christ child. Or Buddhists may turn to Kuan Yin, who is known to come in times of need. If you can see Saint Christopher or another ascended master in your mind's eye when moments of anxiety come—and they will come—you will know that the master will guide you and guard you.

He Will Guide and Guard You Forever

He will guide and guard you forever
He will carry you far in his arms
He hides himself from the clever
He enshrines the poor with His charm.

You may find it more effective if you personalize this mantra: "He will guide and guard *me* forever. He will carry *me* far in his arms.

As we file out of the lecture hall, we hum, "He will guide and guard me forever." And each one of us is planning to experiment with the call to the Electronic Presence of Archangel Michael before we go to sleep. We can visualize his armor over us, his blazing blue-flame sword, his crystalline helmet of pure light substance, his shield, his boots, his gauntlets—everything! And we are also going to remember to call for his protection again when we wake up in the morning.

~ *If you wish to further enhance your study before proceeding to Chapter 20, you will find exercises on p. 235.*

CHAPTER TWENTY

Initiations
of the Divine Mother

Serapis Bey begins his lecture tonight by saying that the ascension flame is the flame of Mother, and the energy that we raise from the base of the spine to the crown is the Mother flame.

The Ascension Flame is the Mother Flame

Our own ascension flame exists as potential within us and forms the nucleus of the base-of-the-spine chakra. In order for that nucleus of energy to be released in consonance with the ascension flame at Luxor, we must transmute all resistance to Mother, all envy of Mother, all fear of Mother and all perversions that block the rising of that flame within us.

God will not allow that flame to rise within us until we are ready, because it would not be beneficial to our life if that flame were released while we still had negative energies pitted against our own Self as Mother or against God as Mother.

This is why it is unsafe for us in the West to practice Kundalini yoga and so raise the great light of the Mother from our base-of-the-spine chakra to connect with the descending light of the Father in the heart chakra, without having first purified the other chakras and released any misqualified energy in them. For as the flame rises, it will contact and reactivate that energy, which could cause a disturbance within us.

The Mother Flame Rising

Serapis Bey tells us that several years ago the temples of Lemuria underneath the Pacific Ocean began to open beneath the waves.

And tonight he would like to explain the importance of this:

"When the Mother flame rises from the depths of Lemuria, from the Great Pyramid, from the citadel of light in your temple, you may anticipate that all that remains within you that is not balanced will also come to the surface. The Mother light brings to the surface all that is within consciousness.

"We, then, are certain that our methods and our training are such that no one will be given an increment of light in whom that light will cause a disturbance that the individual will not be able to deal with. We know the power of the Mother light. We know the Mother light intimately."

In our studies of accountability and the psychology of wholeness, we are told what hard work it takes to tackle every record that is still in our subconscious or unconscious mind, for we have become accustomed to resist some aspect or other of the flame of Mother.

This resistance can show up as a lack of discipline or as sluggishness and self-hatred. It can manifest as lethargy or moodiness or anything from pouting or crying to taking drugs and living a self-destructive lifestyle. All these forms of behavior are really enmity against the Mother light rising from the base chakra. When we step into the ascension flame, we're stepping into the arms of Mother, and we must bring a certain portion of the Mother light to that flame so that our soul will not be consumed.

If we have not garnered within ourselves enough of the ascension fire, then we are not permitted to enter the flame at Luxor. For if we were to stand in the ascension flame right now with our untransmuted karma, our fears, our doubts, our hatred and negativity, our identity would be canceled out. We would be consumed. And so the masters will not allow this initiation to take place until we are prepared.

The ascension flame cannot hurt anyone or anything but darkness. To be able to stand in the ascension flame and become ascended masters, we need to remove all the misused energy that remains within us. Hence the path of initiation.

So we are now preparing for that moment when we can give to Serapis Bey something of our own that we have forged and won—the precious flame of Mother, the precious flame of the ascension.

Relationship with Mother

Let us think a little about our relationship to Mother—the Mother within us as the light of our lives and of the ascension flame, the mother who bore us in this life, the Mother who comes to us in the person of the Guru or Teacher.

Everyone who teaches us, whether male or female, takes on the role of Mother. If people have problems in their relationships to women and especially women in authority, it may well go back to their difficulties with the Mother.

In the same way, problems with figures of authority are often psychological and they extend throughout many lifetimes. We need to resolve our psychology with our human parents as well as with our Divine Parents, for unless we achieve this resolution, we cannot stand in the ascension flame.

The Hail Mary

The path to the ascension can also be seen as a path of devotion to the Father-Mother God. The masters have advised us to choose a lady master, such as Mother Mary or the Bodhisattva Kuan Yin, as the focus of our devotion to the Divine Mother.

If we choose Mother Mary, any antagonism we may have to the Mother may be resolved by giving the Hail Mary. For when Mother Mary comes into our temple in response to our call, she resolves all misuses of the Mother light, the white light of purity.

We can identify with Mary much more easily than we can with the Universal Mother, so we can give our devotion to her as the representative of the Universal Mother. And as we give our love to her as Mother, we will also learn to see ourselves as Mother.

We truly need to resolve our relationship with the Mother, and each time we give our devotion to Mother Mary, the ascension flame rises within us. Giving the Hail Mary is thus the safest way to practice Kundalini yoga.

> Hail, Mary, full of grace
>   the Lord is with thee.
> Blessed art thou among women
>   and blessed is the fruit
>   of thy womb, Jesus.

> Holy Mary, Mother of God
> Pray for us, sons and daughters of God
> Now and at the hour of our victory
> Over sin, disease, and death.

Completion of Spirals

Serapis would like us to turn to an initiation called "the completion of spirals," which explains to us why we need to finish what we start. People may spend lifetime after lifetime dealing with this, for they have often neglected to finish what they start and as a result they feel obliged to make excuses for themselves. Their actions can even cause them to live in the midst of chaos and confusion, which as a misuse of time and energy is also a perversion of the Mother flame.

Serapis explains: "If, then, there is failure or defeat or a lack of completion in your life, realize that this is a disease of the four lower bodies, the disease of lack of fulfillment. And I call it a disease because there is no worse travesty of the law than that of incomplete action.

"Lack of fulfillment of the rituals in matter will, surely as I live, deprive you of union with ascension's flame. Understand that the waste of time and energy, the dissipation of energies through disorganization, indulgences and every form of intrusion upon the mind of Christ is, in one aspect or another, a form of selfishness. It is an attention in some way to the not-self when the attention should be riveted on the Divine Self.

"And so I say, whatever you do, before you begin to do it,

decide well that this is a project that is worthy of God's energy, of your time and space, of your allotment in this life. And when you have decided that this project fits in with cosmic purpose, with the goal of the ascension, with your service to God and man, then plan it well.

"Day by day give invocations to the flame of the ascension for the release of the energy to nourish your project, to integrate energies, to organize your time, your mind and the flow of life within you. And see to it, then, that once you have determined that this project is a part of your blueprint of life, that it is your divine plan, let nothing deter you from its fulfillment.

"For when you fail to complete a cycle, you have failed the Divine Mother. You have failed the test of the feminine ray, of Omega and her energies that are always for the fulfillment of the thrust of Alpha, of Spirit, of Father.

"In this age now precipitating the cycles of Aquarius, remember that this is the time for the fulfillment of the Divine Feminine within you. And above all, it is a time when you dare not fail the Mother, the Mother flame, by failing to conclude each cycle that is begun as a spiral within you from your heart.

"When you put aside those goals that you have determined are the will of God, it is usually for some concern or involvement that centers around a self, whether yours or anothers, through some form of sympathy or the attempt of the fallen ones to disorganize or overthrow your project.

"You must, however, allow for the evolution of the mind of Christ and for the will of God within your project. Submit your project to the will of God, and ask the LORD of Hosts to improve upon the design and the plan and the release of those energies as you are able to increase your vision of the ultimate fulfillment of the goal. And, therefore, in the alchemy of the spirit, there is room for creative expansion of an idea.

"If you make invocations to the crystal-fire mist of the white light, together with the emerald ray from the heart of Cyclopea, who is the All-Seeing Eye of God, you will find day by day that definitions of worthy goals and means of reaching those goals will be released to you. And then you will be aware of the assignment that is yours to fulfill as a part of your divine plan in this lifetime. For it is absolute law that you cannot be given a test for which you have not been given preparation.

"Remember, then, that to accept an assignment is to sign your name in the Book of Life for the ultimate fulfillment of that assignment. Heaven will not accept failure when you have put your name and your pledge and your energy to an assignment you are expected to fulfill. This is the law. This is the action of the ascension flame."

There is a moment of silence as Serapis Bey finishes his instruction. We feel somewhat overwhelmed as we try to process this latest teaching. Serapis turns to us: "Beloved ones, I realize that I have given you some very serious material tonight. I don't want you to be burdened, but it is important that I explain these concepts to you.

"Even if you haven't visited a Catholic Church in this lifetime, your soul knows Mother Mary as one who has loved you throughout the ages. Practice saying the Hail Mary many times a day and see how additional insights about your ascension will come to you.

"The initiation concerning the completion of spirals is one that must be passed before you can stand in the ascension flame. If you are a person who is inclined to be 'scattered' or 'spaced out,' pray for the integration of your four lower bodies. And if procrastination is a problem in your life, remember that El Morya said, 'Procrastination is a disease that is the death of the disciple.' He also said, 'Your spirituality is expressed by your practicality.'

"Call to us, dear hearts, and we will help you pass your initiations. Good night, one and all."

∻ *If you wish to further enhance your study before proceeding to Chapter 21, you will find exercises on p. 235.*

🌿

CHAPTER TWENTY-ONE

The Initiatic Path to the Ascension

*S*erapis opens our class by saying, *"I hope you feel more at peace than when I left you last evening. It takes time to comprehend all the initiations that must be passed before you can fulfill the requirements for the ascension.*

"The final major initiations on the path to the ascension are the transfiguration, the crucifixion, the resurrection and finally the ascension itself. I will discuss these a little later at the conclusion of our series of lectures, but now I would like to summarize the initiations we have discussed thus far."

A Short Review

We have discussed the ascension and the Ascension Retreat, understanding ourselves, the removal of tension and the necessity for maintaining harmony in our world. We have learned how to put an end to struggle by applying Saint Germain's teaching that the sense of struggle makes the struggle.

We have considered the need for surrender and how to truly say that we want the will of God in our lives. We have discussed how to become a friend of God as Abraham was. Then we talked about selfishness, depression, loneliness and anxiety as forms of selfishness, for they show too much concern for the little self.

We talked about the art of becoming childlike and the initiation of nonattachment, which is a difficult one and one of the Buddhic initiations. We spoke of nonattachment to the fruits of our actions, to our desires and to our families.

Lord Lanto told us about the electronic belt and about the effect of our moods. We heard about the initiation of not reacting to the moods of others and we discussed our ego and the trouble it can get us into until we're able to exchange it for the Divine Ego.

We talked about the completion of spirals and the penalty we pay for incomplete action. We discussed self-condemnation and how it can drain us of our energy. We looked at our need to overcome fear and doubt as well as our inability to forgive, and we saw how difficult these tests are to pass.

We studied the initiations of the Mother and how the Hail Mary can help us attain resolution with her. We saw how we needed to resolve our conflicts with our mother in this life and although it doesn't matter whether our mother responds to us, we must be able to completely forgive her for anything we may have held against her as a child or as an adult.

It is not enough for us to just be aware of these initiations, for if we are sincere about wanting our ascension, we must work hard to overcome the negative qualities that remain in our world. Remember, Lord Lanto says, "It is not what you know that counts, but what you do."

Attunement

One more initiation that we must examine is the ability to be in constant attunement with God. Mother Mary has told us that we need this attunement so that when emergencies arise, the masters can immediately move in to help us. "If you are not in attunement with God at all times," she said, "how can he act for you in time of danger or crisis or opposition?

"It means that in the presence of danger you must first make your attunement before you can receive assistance. In the life of a disciple there is not time for this, beloved ones.

"Attunement must be ready as an armor, as a sword of truth. When you are in a battle, you can not run back to the lines and put on your armor and your sword after the enemy has launched their attack. There you must be ready.

"Attunement, therefore, is somewhat of a subconscious

quality. It is begun with the outer mind; it is begun by its suppli-cation, by the prayer to the Holy Christ Self to take command and continue the prayers and decrees of your heart throughout the entire twenty-four hours. This is an important request.

"Realize that you can utter simple prayers all through the day as they are inspired upon your heart by your own Holy Christ Self who is indeed praying before the Father twenty-four hours a day. And then accept this in full faith, beloved ones, and realize that the hierarchy of light may take over your form, your world. You no longer need to feel that at any moment in the day you must first approach God, for you are already one with him.

"And thus, no situation that comes to you will take you off guard, for you will be on guard in the vanguard of light. This is the requirement of the hour. Do not underestimate your service to the light, and realize that one with God is a majority for the entire planetary body.

"To feel the attunement with the Holy Spirit at all times is something which was taught to me before I could be given the opportunity to bear the Christ and assist him in his mission. I would like to give you a prayer that will help you maintain your attunement at all times."

> *Beloved mighty I AM Presence, Father of all Life,*
>   *Act on my behalf this day:*
>
> *Fill my form.*
>
> *Release the Light that is necessary*
>   *For me to go forth to do thy will,*
>
> *And see that at every hand the decisions I make*
>   *Are according to thy holy will.*
>
> *See that my energies are used to magnify the* LORD
>   *In everyone whom I meet.*
>
> *See to it that thy holy wisdom released to me*
>   *Is used constructively for the expansion of God's kingdom.*

And above all, beloved Heavenly Father,
  I commend my spirit unto thee

And ask that as thy Flame is one with my Flame,
  The union of these two Flames shall pulsate

To effect in my world
  The continuous alertness and attunement

Which I need with thy Holy Presence,
  With the Holy Spirit, and with the World Mother.[1]

The best way to explain attunement is again in banking terms. We have two types of bank accounts, our checking account and our savings account. We can withdraw funds at any time from our checking account but we have placed money in advance in our savings account so that when a need for a larger amount arises, we will have the money available.

Before we can withdraw funds from either of these accounts, we must have first deposited our money in the bank. It's the same with our decrees. As we give our energy to God in our morning and evening decrees, we build up our savings account. Then, if we are suddenly in need of help as our car starts to skid, we can instantly call to Archangel Michael and he will send his angels to help us bring our car under control or at least keep someone from hitting us.

If we are in attunement with Archangel Michael, we have already built up a relationship with him whereby we feel free, because of our reservoir of blue-flame decrees, to shout, "Lord Michael, help me!" And we can be sure that he will.

At this point, Serapis says, "I would like to stop for a moment and give an opportunity to anyone who would like to speak. Have you any experiences you would like to share with us when the masters saved you from injury?"

One student says, "Once Archangel Michael saved me from a serious accident or death. I was preparing to go to South America on a pilgrimage. I had gone to the store for some last-minute items when a car appeared out of nowhere as I stopped at an intersection. I had no time to do anything except shout, 'Lord Michael!'

"The steering wheel was instantly lifted out of my hand and my car swerved and made a complete arc out of the way of the oncoming car, which only hit my rear bumper. The driver in the oncoming car swore that he had not seen me at that stop sign.

"When the police officer arrived, he said, 'Lady, don't bother about it. It's only a fender bender.' The car was not scratched, but the impact was so loud that neighbors came to look.

"I can personally attest that Archangel Michael is an excellent driver who saved me from serious injury. At the speed at which the other car was traveling, the collision would definitely not have been a 'fender bender' without the intervention of Archangel Michael and his band of blue-flame angels. Thank you, I am truly grateful!"

Serapis thanks the student and we continue with the night's instruction.

Patience

Mother Mary has also told us about the necessity for patience—a difficult initiation for some. She says: "Remember that in this world you must always consider that the manifestation of God is sometimes tempered by time and space. At other times, instantaneous precipitation is possible. Therefore expect the immediate, but be willing to wait in patience in the possession of your souls for the fulfilling of the Divine within you.

"It is true that saints in the past have lost initiations and have failed tests because of impatience. Your patience must be tried, for it is the trying of your faith, the trying of your momentum and your dedication; and this must be tested in all ways.

"The key to opportunity, beloved ones, is the fulfillment of the law of your own being. Until that law is fulfilled, the next cycle of attainment cannot be opened for you."[2]

We must remember that we should not try to bypass initiations in our impatience to reach the goal. We're progressing up a spiral staircase and we cannot jump from step one to step ten. Instead, we should keep advancing step by step, up and up and up. And one more step always lies ahead of us.

Remember that those behind us are waiting for us to move on, to leave that step and to go up higher so that they can move up to where we were. By refusing our initiations we are holding others back, and yet by trying to hurry we may crash into those directly ahead of us!

Competition

If we can conquer the need to be competitive in our daily lives and learn to avoid any form of competition with our business associates, our family or friends, we can achieve a great sense of peace.

The master will often tell us how important it is for disciples on the Path to understand that they are never competing with one another but only with their own momentums. They are striving to overcome by arriving just a little bit ahead of themselves and succeeding where perhaps they had failed before.

We should not be competing with someone who had more money than we did as a child or had a better education then, or has better opportunities now. We should be competing only with ourselves as we progress steadily up the spiral of the ascension. We're not measuring ourselves against the person next to us and worrying about how fast he is going. That's not the point at all. We each have our own path and separate initiations.

Harmony

Maintaining our harmony, although difficult indeed, is absolutely essential if we wish to achieve the goal of the ascension at the end of this lifetime. To be harmonious is to have mastered our emotions and our moods.

Gabriel, the archangel of ascension's flame, tells us that the masters desire to give us more light and more energy but, he says: "It is a question of mathematics. You do not place fifty pounds of lead in a tissue sack. It will break. It will tear. Therefore, fortify your chakras and your lower bodies by the spiritual exercise of harmony."

Harmony is one of the qualities of ascension's ray, so we need to explore it a little more. The great cosmic being called God Harmony has told us: "Harmony is a science, even as music is a science. Harmony is the balance of light, of sun centers, of electronic forcefields. When there is balance, then there is harmony. When there is balance and harmony, then and only then can there be acceleration.

"You may have wondrous gifts of virtue but often in a lifetime, or many lifetimes, an individual does not exceed a certain level of attainment because he reaches the line where there is no longer balance, where he cannot carry into an accelerated momentum a virtue that may function at a lesser vibration.

"Take, for example, a top that spins. In order to spin, it must have a certain acceleration and a certain balance. Thus when the law of harmony functioning within you goes below the level of a certain acceleration, it can no longer be maintained.

"This is when discord enters in with disintegration and ultimately self-destruction. Thus, in order to have the key of harmony, you must have the key of acceleration of love. For example, under normal conditions an individual may express patience or mercy or kindness, but as soon as stress or distress is introduced into his life, then the individual is no longer kind, patient and merciful."

Thus the key to harmony is love, self discipline and patience. A moment in time exists before we give way to anger or any other negative emotion when we can gain control of ourselves if we choose to do so and stop ourselves from acting in a way we might later regret. But this requires vigilance and a true desire to retain our harmony.

How quickly and easily our feeling world can become depressed or excited or angered. How easily emotions become a tempest in a teapot and suddenly the sea begins to roar. This is when we need to still those emotions with the calm words of the Christ in the boat when the sea roared without—"Peace be still and know that I am God." For these energies must be controlled before they control us.

The measure of our God-mastery must be our ability to hold the flame of peace when all assails us, when riptides of human emotion, condemnation or persecution or even outright lies assail us.

Serapis says that there is "a calm center within the heart, there is a center within the secret chamber of the heart and there is a center within the solar-plexus chakra whereby you can maintain peace and not follow the turbulence of the world's turmoil.

"Understand, then, that these are the testings that are repeated day after day until nothing—no thing in this world—is capable of moving you from your fixed attention upon your God Self.

"And what is the formula for this mastery? It is this, quite simply: that you love God and your oneness with him more than you love yourself—loving God and loving to be in his presence, waiting upon the LORD for the next initiation on the path.

"Harmony is the key. And when you can guard your harmony in the face of aggravation, irritation, even lies and calumny, then you will be ready for the acceleration of ascension's flame."

Constancy

Many of the problems that we encounter every day may be unresolved karmic situations from the past. They may be coming up now for redemption in the form of people who are irritating or situations that are seemingly unfair. We must be honest with ourselves and realize that in the past we probably stumbled into situations that caused us to lose control. Now it is up to us to exercise control and to receive these tests with harmony.

Another initiation that must be passed if we are to ascend the pyramid is constancy. Constancy is a quality of the green ray. It means to keep on keeping on; it means persevering when it looks as though everything is going nowhere. And then all of a sudden, through perseverance, through constancy, the entire picture will change and we will see a successful conclusion to a situation that once seemed almost impossible.

Faith enters into this test. Faith and illumination are the components of the flame of constancy. As El Morya has told us, "It matters not how many times you fall. Arise and proceed onward." Remember that Saint Germain told us to be sure to get up one more time than we fall.

Details

The masters have said that as they look at the consciousness of the people on earth, they find that it is a lack of attention to detail that deprives them of their victory. For the path to the ascension is nothing but detail.

Disciples who have the ability to handle details, who leave no stone unturned, who discipline themselves, will have the small victories that make the final victory—just as the raindrops, one by one, make the streams and rivers of life.

Humility

The need for humility is another requirement that may hold back a disciple for many, many lifetimes. We may be stuck on this initiation and not be aware of how many times we have kept coming back into embodiment because we failed to pass this test. We are told that when Jesus came to Luxor, Serapis felt that Jesus should initiate him. "No," said Jesus. "I want to start right at the beginning."

Thus Jesus was the epitome of the quality of humility when he asked to start at the bottom of the spiral, even though he merited the very highest initiations.

Serapis says: "If pride remains, it doth indeed go before the fall of that individual into numerous pitfalls. These pitfalls are subtle, involving the character of the self. I urge upon all, then, that they seek the banner of divine humility.

"If the masters have ever recognized any of the errors of men that have hindered them from becoming that which they long to become, they have recognized their pride. Pride takes many forms and true humility but one.

"True humility must be worn eternally. It is not a garment you place upon yourself for a moment, for a day or a year or when passing a test. It is an undergarment with which God himself is clothed, and unless it surround thee, thy hopes of attainment are slim indeed." [3]

Joy

The requirement to live in the flame of joy seems so natural but turns out to be quite difficult. People seem to have passed by the flame of joy that the masters tell us is the antithesis of sorrow. Serapis says, "Like a beautiful and splendid mountain stream, the joy of God flows forth into the world every day. It sparkles and runs over the rocks and impediments. It leaps in the sunlight. It is happy because the joy of God knows nothing but purity, nothing but perfection. It sparkles like diamonds. It flows forth from eternity's fountainhead. And it is accepted by the hearts of the saints. They welcome it with joy. They reach down their hands and thirstily they drink of this fountain."

We can go through life bowed down by the troubles we face or we can rise above them and transcend them. If we transcend them, we will be living that much closer to our divine Presence, our Real Self, and we will no longer be overwhelmed by the sorrows of everyday life.

To accept that the joy of God is everywhere may be the one thing that has been missing in our lives. Just plain joy—vibrant joy, joy in self, joy in nature, joy in opportunity, joy in art and joy even in the process of purifying oneself and preparing for the ascension.

Along with joy comes thankfulness and many other positive emotions. Look back and see if there has been a twenty-four-hour period recently where you remained joyful the entire time. You might try this for the next twenty-four hours and find to your surprise that you have broken out of the gloom-and-doom consciousness worn by many in today's world.

∴ *If you wish to further enhance your study before proceeding to Chapter 22, you will find exercises on p. 237.*

❦

CHAPTER TWENTY-TWO

Bodies Terrestrial and Bodies Celestial

Serapis tells us that this class will be short but necessary. He points out that today the question often arises as to how to dispose of the body after death. People have much anxiety about the passing of loved ones on this planet and the various religions have many differing beliefs.

How to Help the Soul Make Her Transition

After death, whether the soul ascends or prepares at inner levels for reembodiment, the physical body must pass through the natural process of dissolution. Therefore, in order to facilitate the soul's transition to higher octaves, the ascended masters recommend that the body be placed on ice for a period of two days and two nights. It should then be cremated on the third day.

Most funeral parlors will carry out this request. Dry ice may be used or, if that is not possible, the body may be kept refrigerated. On the third day, if they themselves do not have one, the mortuary will take the body to the crematorium. The third day is the day when Jesus was resurrected. So waiting three days commemorates the time he spent in the tomb.

Family members and friends may gather at the crematorium to make calls for the soul to be taken to the octaves of light and to be cut free from the astral plane. They should also make calls for the light to be withdrawn from the body, for as long as light remains in the body it binds the soul to earth. Through cremation, the light is returned to the etheric plane. Thus the soul has now no reason to remain tied to the earth.

Often a memorial service is held shortly after cremation.

At this time it is important to make calls that the soul of the departed loved one be taken to the appropriate place for her evolution. We should pray that the angels take her to the schoolroom where she can make the best progress. A simple call can be made to the angels of Archangel Michael and the Elohim Astrea to escort the soul to the retreats of learning or to a place of temporary rest if she has passed on in great pain or trauma.

Due to custom and the mistaken concept that the physical body will be raised at the second coming of Christ, many people have chosen to bury the bodies of their loved ones at the close of this life, for they believe that cremation prevents the resurrection of the body.

But the masters teach that the physical body does not enter in to the resurrection, rather it is the soul that is resurrected in a spiritual body. Consequently, the preservation of the physical form for the life to come is unnecessary.

On the day of the resurrection when Christ shall summon the elect to rise from the earth, they shall arise in new garments, new light bodies, and they shall indeed be with him in the great rapture of the Lord.

Embalming

Embalming is a means of further prolonging the soul's bondage to form; therefore, the masters definitely do not recommend that the body be embalmed. When this occurs, the blood is removed and discarded as waste and thus is not consigned to the flames. Since the blood carries the light and the identity pattern of the soul, which cannot be separated from the body except by fire, it is wise to see that the body is preserved intact as it is placed on ice.

Autopsy

The Masters do not recommend an autopsy unless there has been foul play, or a question arises as to the cause of death. However, if an autopsy is necessary, it is wise to insist that all the organs disturbed during the autopsy be placed with the body in the cremation ritual.

It is important that we make a will and that our families be aware of our wishes. Nevertheless, occasionally a family member may override the written will and choose to proceed with embalming and burial rather than cremation.

If this should happen, we should remember that the power of the Holy Spirit when invoked through the violet flame is able to transmute cause, effect, record and memory of all that is left of the physical self, wherever it may be in the earth's crust. Truly, the universal grace of God is sufficient for man's salvation.

~ *If you wish to further enhance your study before proceeding to Chapter 23, you will find exercises on p. 237.*

CHAPTER TWENTY-THREE

The Initiations of the Transfiguration, Crucifixion and Resurrection

Serapis says, "I can now give you a glimpse of ascension's glory."

The Initiation of the Transfiguration

We have arrived at the three final initiations preceding that of the ascension itself. The transfiguration occurs when the light within every cell and atom of the body expands as that light contacts the light of God in the universe. As the disciple magnetizes the light within him and surrenders his darkness into the light, every cell and atom within his form becomes sealed in the light. As the light within merges with the light without, the disciple is transfigured and sealed in his new level of attainment. In that instant he becomes a body of light.

When we are transfigured we put off our old consciousness of the sense of sin, selfishness, self-condemnation and lack of self-worth. We take off that old garment and put on the robe of the living Christ.

The recounting of Jesus' transfiguration in Matthew 17:1–9 is given so that we may understand that this glorious initiation can one day come to us all.

And after six days Jesus taketh Peter, James, and John his brother, and bringeth them up into an high mountain apart,

And was transfigured before them: and his face did shine as the sun, and his raiment was white as the light.

And, behold, there appeared unto them Moses and Elias talking with him.

Then answered Peter and said unto Jesus, Lord, it is good for us to be here: if thou wilt, let us make here three tabernacles; one for thee and one for Moses and one for Elias.

While he yet spake, behold, a bright cloud overshadowed them: and behold a voice out of the cloud which said, This is my beloved Son in whom I am well pleased; hear ye him.

And when the disciples heard it, they fell on their face and were sore afraid.

And Jesus came and touched them and said, Arise, and be not afraid.

And when they had lifted up their eyes, they saw no man, save Jesus only.

And as they came down from the mountain, Jesus charged them, saying, Tell the vision to no man until the Son of man be risen again from the dead.

When Jesus took Peter, James and John apart and was transfigured before them, it was the prelude to his resurrection and his ascension. It was the celebration of the light in his heart filling all his temple, even the very cells of his being.

And so we contemplate the words of Jesus recorded in the Gospel of Mark: "Verily I say unto you, that there be some of them that stand here which shall not taste of death till they have seen the kingdom of God come with power." Mark wrote this preceding his description of the transfiguration.

It is a tremendous prophecy of the power of God's light with us today. It means that we need not pass through the transition called death before we have gained access to the kingdom of God and have internalized its light.

God's kingdom is his consciousness. It is all-light, all-power, all-wisdom and all-love. It is the Trinity in manifestation—yours to claim through the divine spark of your God-identity—the threefold flame in your heart. It is yours to exercise through the science of the spoken Word.

Here is a prayer on the transfiguration for your own self-transformation. As you give this prayer, see yourself stepping out of your old garments of limitation and putting on the shining garment of the Christ. See yourself filled with light. Feel yourself becoming "shining, exceeding white as snow," as we read in the Gospel of Mark.

Transfiguration

I AM changing all my garments,
Old ones for the bright new day;
With the sun of understanding
I AM shining all the way.

I AM light within, without;
I AM light is all about.
Fill me, free me, glorify me,
Seal me, heal me, purify me!
Until transfigured they describe me
I AM shining like the Son,
I am shining like the sun!

The Initiation of the Crucifixion

Remember that Paul told us, "I die daily." We must follow him by dying daily to our human will, our human ego and our human intellect so that we can resurrect ourselves in the Christ. Within us is a Higher Self in Christ, our Higher Mental Body that can contain the Mind of God. When we let go of our human will, intellect and ego, we can put on the Christ consciousness.

El Morya and Lanello have both told us not to "try to perfect the human, but to replace it with the Christ." We are letting our human self die on that cross and replacing it by our Christ Self. Our aim is to walk the earth with the Christ Mind resurrected in us rather than trying to perfect our human self.

We Are Not Meant to Die on the Cross— We Are Meant to Live

Serapis says, "I have invited John the Beloved to speak to us about the crucifixion—our own personal crucifixion, resurrection and ascension. He is well qualified to speak about these subjects since he was the beloved disciple who was so close to the Master Jesus.

"John witnessed Jesus' initiations during that lifetime and was with him at the foot of the cross. His love for the master was so great that with Mary and Martha, he also stayed to see Jesus endure the crucifixion. John was there on resurrection morning also, experiencing the glory of the resurrection fires. He saw his master ascend into the cloud, as did the five hundred, from Bethany's hill."

John greets us and begins to speak.

"Do you understand that you can pass through this initiation of the crucifixion without surrendering the four lower bodies?

"Do you understand that the atonement that you can make is an atonement of energy, whereby through the surrender of all the energy that God has ever given you into the flame of the sacred fire, you can hold the balance for the planet by the weight of light? You can say, 'My burden is light.' For the burden of light that you carry comes from the sacrifice of all that is less than perfection.

"There are some in every age who elect to become stars in the firmament of being. As one age is concluded and another begins, there must be those who make the arc, carrying energy spirals from one dispensation to the next, from one level of consciousness to the next. These form the bridge over which all of humanity pass into the golden age of enlightenment and peace.

"The initiation of the crucifixion involves the descent of the soul to the darkest levels of the planet where those rebellious ones are who have refused to acknowledge the Christ. Therefore, while the body of Jesus lay in the tomb, his soul and his higher mind were active in the depths of the astral plane, in the place that has been called purgatory.

"This is where the souls of the departed ones from the

days of Noah, the days of the sinking of Atlantis, were held because they refused to submit to the law of God. They had, until recently, been denied rebirth and entrance to the screen of life."

John is telling us that Jesus' life demonstrated his acceptance of the assignment of the crucifixion. However, we are not meant to die on the cross, we are meant to live. We must go through the same initiation that Jesus did, but we do not have to physically die.

We are meant to go on living as an example for others on the Path. What we place on the cross is our lower nature and that is the sacrifice that God expects of us in this age rather than the death of our body.

The age of transition John was speaking of is where we are now. As the Piscean age closes, the Aquarian age opens, and we must form the bridge from Jesus' dispensation in the Piscean age to that of Saint Germain's in the age of Aquarius.

Today many of us are fulfilling the requirement of the crucifixion as we work with the homeless and attempt to rehabilitate those who are suffering from AIDS, alcohol and drug abuse, or who are victims of poverty, hunger, crime—all the myriad problems in our society today.

Without the Cross There Can Be No Crown

John the Beloved says that he would like to give us one sentence that sums up the initiation of the crucifixion. It is "Without the cross there can be no crown; without the crucifixion there can be no resurrection." When our time of testing comes and we fear that we may give way, we must remember the victorious ones who have gone before us, showing us that we can be victorious also. We shall overcome.

If we think of our earlier example of mountain climbing, we will remember that we are hikers in the Himalayas in the midst of a blizzard, surrounded by snow, sleet and ice, and we dare not let the rope slacken that links us to those behind us. If we do, they will fall.

Serapis Bey closes his instruction with some words of love. He says, "My hands will be extended in loving welcome to thee at the hour of thy victory. I remain your teacher and friend, Serapis Bey."

The Initiation of the Resurrection

The initiation of the resurrection takes place when we receive into our form the regenerative energy of God—an energy that possesses the capacity to quicken our atoms and our electrons and reenergize our form.

Starting with the ritual of the transfiguration, the flame rises within us and brings our energies into alignment with the energies of the Christ. The resurrection flame itself flows through our bodies when we receive this initiation. It is the color of opalescent milky-white mother-of-pearl and contains within it all the colors of the threefold flame—blue, yellow and pink.

The vibratory rate of the resurrection flame is higher than that of the threefold flame, for in it the colors whirl faster and faster until they attain a lustrous, mother-of-pearl radiance. Then it continues to vibrate faster and faster until it becomes the pure white light of the ascension flame.

Saint Germain gave us a beautiful explanation of the resurrection. He said: "There is a destiny that you perceive when you poke your head above the clouds of human creation, and that destiny is the destiny of the soul of a people in Aquarius and of your own soul. Apart from all that surrounds you, there is that inner life and inner walk with God and there is that determination, above all, to attain that reunion with your Mighty I AM Presence in this life which is the victory of the ascension.

"I adjure you: Never lose sight of the goal! For if you desire to help this planet and not to desert her in her hour of trouble, then remember, the light that you carry prior to the ascension and after is the means of effecting a great alchemy, a world chemicalization. The resurrection is a resurgence of light in the physical temple whereby you walk the earth in physical bodies, yet bearing the flame of the resurrection, a spiral of mother-of-pearl radiance whereby the rainbow rays of God are emitted from you.

"The resurrection of the soul, then, is her restoration to the heart of the inner light, the inner Christ, the inner Buddha. The resurrection is a goal to be realized not after death but before it. And it is the absorption of that light of restoration whereby the Lord did say, 'Behold, I make all things new.' "[1]

Let us add here that we do believe we can receive the initiation of the resurrection without having to go through the process called death. Initiates who are in the resurrected state walk the earth today. The masters need some of us to be their hands and feet and those over whom they can place their Electronic Presence as we become their representatives in form.

I AM the Resurrection and the Life

We may invoke the resurrection flame right now through a wonderful mantra that Jesus brought back from the Himalayas. In his so-called lost years he studied there from the age of twelve until he was twenty-nine, and he received this mantra from his guru, Lord Maitreya: "I AM the resurrection and the life."[2]

We should keep this affirmation at the forefront of our mind and use it for whatever problem lies before us, saying: "I AM, I AM, I AM the resurrection and the life." And after these words, we can add anything we like that is the need of the moment. For example, "I AM the resurrection and the life of my health, my finances, my business, my marriage, my family, my studies"— anything that needs attention in our lives.

When we give this affirmation, the resurrection flame passes through us. It resurrects our memory, our mental faculties, our desire to know God. It rejuvenates our being and it resurrects the memory of our divine plan. It's one of the most wonderful flames we can invoke.

Resurrection

I AM the flame of resurrection
Blazing God's pure light through me.
Now I AM raising every atom,
From every shadow I AM free.

I AM the light of God's full presence,
I AM living ever free.
Now the flame of life eternal
Rises up to victory.

*If you wish to further enhance your study before proceeding
to Chapter 24, you will find exercises on p. 237.*

CHAPTER TWENTY-FOUR

🌿

The Initiation of the Ascension

Serapis begins: "Now we come to the final initiation of the ascension. Keep on striving to attain your goal. Keep your eyes firmly fixed on the promise of your ascension, no matter how much you may feel buffeted by life. And never forget to call to us for help. We are waiting for your permission to enter your world and teach you further truths from our ascended master octave.

"Let me return to some ideas that I gave earlier and that I feel you still need to consider.

"Immortality is of a high price, and it demands the all-ness of men from the smallness of men. Men cannot build out of mortal substance immortal bodies. They cannot build out of mortal feelings divine feelings that enfold the world and create the Great Pyramid of Life. The flame of the ascension is the key that unlocks the door to immortality for every man.[1]

"It is written in the Book of Life, 'No man shall see God and live.' For when God stands in the presence of man, man can no longer live as man but must live as God. And if he refuses to live as God, then that portion of consciousness which posed itself as a separate identity from God must be no more, for it is consumed upon contact with the very fire of God's being.

"It is absolutely essential that you know, in the final analysis, that you and you alone shall pass through that doorway, for no one can pass through the doorway of Cosmic Christ purity for you. No one can attain to the manifestation of eternal victory and righteousness.

"In Reality there is no past and no future. There is only the present moment. And with the ascension, the last enemy, *or death, is destroyed. Fear not to enter the flame, for you lose nothing but the not self and gain the allness of the Real Self."*

It Is Finished

Jesus has given us a prayer called "It Is Finished!" He bore the karma for the world and for each of us individually throughout the age of Pisces. Now the responsibility has been placed on us. How long will it be before you, too, are willing to say, "It is finished! Done with this episode in strife?"

It Is Finished!
by Jesus the Christ

It is finished!
Done with this episode in strife,
I AM made one with immortal life.
Calmly I AM resurrecting my spiritual energies
From the great treasure-house of immortal knowing.
The days I knew with thee, O Father,
Before the world was—the days of triumph,
When all of the thoughts of thy being
Soared over the ageless hills of cosmic memory;
Come again as I meditate upon thee.
Each day as I call forth thy memories
From the scroll of immortal Love,
I AM thrilled anew.
Patterns wondrous to behold enthrall me
With the wisdom of thy creative scheme.
So fearfully and wonderfully am I made
That none can mar thy design,
None can despoil the beauty of thy holiness,
None can discourage the beating of my heart
In almost wild anticipation
Of thy fullness made manifest within me.

O great and glorious Father,
How shall a tiny bird created in hierarchical bliss
Elude thy compassionate attention?

I AM of greater value than many birds
And therefore do I know that thy loving thoughts
Reach out to me each day
To console me in seeming aloneness,
To raise my courage,
Elevate my concepts,
Exalt my character,
Flood my being with virtue and power,
Sustain thy cup of life flowing over within me,
And abide within me forever
In the nearness of thy heavenly presence.

I cannot fail,
Because I AM thyself in action everywhere.
I ride with thee
Upon the mantle of the clouds.
I walk with thee
Upon the waves and crests of water's abundance.
I move with thee
In the undulations of thy currents
Passing over the thousands of hills
    composing earth's crust.
I AM alive with thee
In each bush, flower and blade of grass.
All nature sings in thee and me,
For we are one.
I AM alive in the hearts of the downtrodden,
Raising them up.
I AM the law exacting the truth of being
In the hearts of the proud,
Debasing the human creation therein
And spurring the search for thy reality.
I AM all things of bliss
To all people of peace.
I AM the full facility of divine grace,
The Spirit of Holiness
Releasing all hearts from bondage into unity.

It is finished!
Thy perfect creation is within me.
Immortally lovely,
It cannot be denied the blessedness of being.
Like unto thyself, it abides in the house of reality.
Nevermore to go out into profanity,
It knows only the wonders of purity and victory.
Yet there stirs within this immortal fire
A consummate pattern of mercy and compassion
Seeking to save forever that which is lost
Through wandering away
From the beauty of reality and truth.
I AM the living Christ in action evermore!

It is finished!
Death and human concepts have no power in my world!
I AM sealed by God-design
With the fullness of that Christ-love
That overcomes, transcends, and frees the world
By the power of the three-times-three
Until all the world is God-victorious—
Ascended in the light and free!

It is finished!
Completeness is the allness of God.
Day unto day an increase of strength, devotion,
Life, beauty, and holiness occurs within me,
Released from the fairest flower of my being,
The Christ-consecrated rose of Sharon
Unfolding its petals within my heart.
My heart is the heart of God!
My heart is the heart of the world!
My heart is the heart of Christ in healing action!
Lo, I AM with you alway, even unto the end,
When with the voice of immortal love
I too shall say, "It is finished!" [2]

Initiates who are candidates for the ascension will often journey to Luxor in their finer bodies to make preparations for the ascension at the conclusion of their final incarnation. They may stay there for hours, days, weeks, months or years before they are given the opportunity to take their ascension from inner levels.

Others who have served God and balanced more than 51 percent of their karma and who have been associated with the holding of the balance of a certain geographical area are often assigned to ascend from the place where they have been serving.

The Wedding Garment

The parable of the wedding garment reveals Jesus' teaching on the spiritual body that we must weave and put on for our ascension.[3] As we invoke the holy energies of God in prayer and service, we spin a body of light out of energy from the heart of our God Presence, called the Deathless Solar Body. We will use this garment of light to carry us up into the higher octaves when we ascend.

Serapis tells us that "only the purified energies of the heart can be returned to the heart of the Presence so that God can actually create a garment of pure light with which the ascending soul may be clothed.

"This garment of light possesses the power of levitation but it also possesses conformity to the outer and Inner Self. It conforms to the Inner Self because it is spun from the energies of God and the original pristine pattern of God for each lifestream.

"Thus the flame above (in the heart of the Presence) magnetizes the flame below (the threefold flame within the heart of the initiate), and the wedding garment descends around the crystal cord to envelop the lifestream of the individual in those tangible and vital currents of the ascension."[4]

We have been told that in the retreats the masters hold classes on how to weave the seamless garment and teach us there that our thoughts, feelings and purified consciousness form the substance of the cloth. One of the ascension angels said: "You would be surprised how many times the initiates must start again and again because of the unevenness of the lines and the threads—the very threads themselves representing the consciousness, the thoughts, the feelings.

"Thoughts are the warp, feelings are the woof, and the fire of the etheric body is the smoothness of the cloth that is to drape as a forcefield of auric protection around the physical body and all of the bodies.

"Some of you who have taken sewing classes, who have found yourselves sewing and then undoing and then sewing and undoing again, can well understand the patience that is required when working on the seamless garment. And the masters of the ascension temple have a very sharp eye for the quality of the garment. They never, never let pass an imperfection in the weave."

Let us make our decision now and resolve with the full fervor of our being to make our ascension. We may say: "LORD, I desire to return to the white fire core of being if that is my divine plan. And I will do a novena to the Great Divine Director to find out God's will for me.*

"I wish to fully embrace the path to the ascension and I am willing to start with the basic initiations. I will slay all that I know is not right in my world and surrender all that is not ready to stand in the ascension flame. Therefore, I am ready to embark on this Path. So help me God."

The Ascension Prayer

I AM ascension light,
Victory flowing free,
All of good won at last
For all eternity.

I AM light, all weights are gone.
Into the air I raise;
To all I pour with full God-power
My wondrous song of praise.

*See Chapter 18 for instruction on the Great Divine Director's Novena.

All hail! I AM the living Christ,
The ever-loving One.
Ascended now with full God-power,
I AM a blazing sun.

The Prodigal Son

You might want to read the parable of the Prodigal Son, for if you consider this parable in the light of the ascension, you may realize that it is the story of a soul who has wandered off the path for many lifetimes and now has finally decided to accept the fires of ascension's flame and return home to the Father.[5]

Serapis Bey gives us a prayer about the prodigal son that he included in the *Dossier on the Ascension.*

O God, here am I, here I AM!
One with thee and one to command
Open the doorway of my consciousness
And let me demand as never before
My birthright to restore.
Thy prodigal son has come to thee
And longs once again to walk with thee
Every step of the way Home.

Serapis would woo us home to God. He tells us that we can truly be transformed by the path to the ascension. "Consciousness can move. It can penetrate. It can fly. It can loose itself from the moorings of life and go out into the sea, the briny deep where the salt tears of my joy are a spume of hope, renewed again and again. I am gladdened as never before, and there is no remembrance of the former conditions. These are put aside as finite, as trite, as a passing fancy of the mortal mind.

"The ascension is an inevitable part of the divine system. It consists of these initiations: the transfiguration into the divine configuration, the ritual of the crucifixion upon the cross of matter, the resurrection from dead substance and the ascension itself, which raises man out of the domain of his recalcitrant energies and all treacherous activities, mortal imperfection and error. The ascension is the beginning of the kingdom for each one. And when every soul is taken and none left, the world itself will ascend back to the heart of God, a planet victorious."6

The Ascension

Serapis tells us that he is rapidly bringing our class to a close and that these are his final instructions:

"I hope, if I can convey nothing else to you, that I can help you to realize that you are worthy of your ascension. I sincerely hope that you can accept the great love and assistance given you by the ascended masters and their teachings.

"Each time one individual returns to the heart of God in the ritual of the ascension, the momentum of that victory is stamped upon all who remain. The ascension flame is more than a flame of white fire—it is a thing of joy and beauty forever. It is an endless visualization, constantly moving, constantly rising, constantly changing, spiraling upward.

"Remember that in the hour of your ascension you will hear issuing out of the flame of the ascension anchored at Luxor the most magnificent rendition of the 'Triumphal March' from Verdi's opera Aïda.

*"It is your victory march! Each time you hear these trumpets, know that it commemorates the moment when you will step onto a dais in the center of the Ascension Temple. With seraphim surrounding the dais and all the brothers and sisters of the Ascension Temple encircling you, you will rise in the ritual of the ascension—*an Ascended Master! Immortal!*"*

:~ *If you wish to further enhance your study you will find exercises on p. 238.*

The trek upward is worth the inconvenience.

—*El Morya*

The Path to Your Ascension

WORKBOOK

*I*t has been said, "When the pupil is ready, the teacher appears." As you read this book, you may find that the material is familiar to you, for you have already prepared yourself in the past and are now ready to enter into a direct relationship with one or more of the ascended masters.

To further facilitate your study, I have prepared a series of exercises to supplement the information given in the text. You may want to read through the book once to familiarize yourself with the steps to the ascension, then turn to these supplemental pages as you reread the individual chapters and meditate on what each chapter means to you. You might also want to keep a notebook and add your insights to it as you go along.

On page 253 you will find a bibliography of books and tapes and following this I have included a glossary of spiritual or esoteric words. In addition, you may want to commune with your God Presence as you read the text, and you may ask the ascended masters to teach you directly or indirectly, as they choose.

Whether or not you do the exercises, you will want to ask each night before you retire for your soul to be taken to the ascended master retreats for further instruction. Here you can attend classes at inner levels while you sleep (just as we did throughout this book).

In *The Chela and the Path: Keys to Soul Mastery in the Aquarian Age*, the Ascended Master El Morya gives us a formula we can use to travel to the retreats. He explains that we can travel to other ascended masters' retreats by inserting the name of the master of our choice. If you make the follow-ing invocation before you retire, the angels will take you to El Morya's retreat in Darjeeling, India:

In the name of the Christ, my own Real Self, I call to

the heart of the I AM Presence and to the angel of the Presence to take me in my soul and in my soul consciousness to the Retreat of God's Will in Darjeeling.

I ask that my four lower bodies be charged and recharged with the will of God and the blueprint for my fulfillment of that will. I ask that I be given the formula for my victory. And I ask that all information necessary for the fulfillment of my divine plan be released to my outer waking consciousness as it is required. I thank thee and I accept it done in the full power of the risen Christ.

Chapter One

1. What does "immortality" mean to you?

2. What is the purpose of your life? Have you defined your goals specifically and made plans to fulfill them within a certain timeframe?

> For many years I have had a sign over my desk that reads: "The ascension: The goal of life." It is in a position where I see it many times a day. Often it helps to have a visual reminder of our goal.

3. Is one of your goals to become an ascended master?

> I have been able to number among my friends several who have ascended. The process of the ascension is not an impersonal event but is actually happening today. I desire with all my heart to someday become an ascended master, if God wills it, and I want as many of you as possible to receive these truths so that you can also ascend.

4. What does the following quote by Serapis mean to you?

> "The future is what you make it, even as the present is what you made it. If you do not like it, God has provided a way for you to change it, and the way is through the acceptance of the currents of the ascension flame."

Do you know of incidents in your life that were influenced by past events?

> *When I first heard this teaching from Serapis Bey, it was as though a light had gone on in my consciousness. I thought, "Ah! That explains many things I have always wondered about." By the grace of God, I have had a fairly satisfactory present life, and I learned to my surprise that I had few trying experiences because of a certain amount of good karma brought over from past lives.*
>
> *Therefore, when I heard that "the future is what you make it," I decided right then and there that my future was going to be the ascension. And I determined at that moment to make the ascension the goal of my life and to work toward it unceasingly.*

5. Is the concept of the ascension new to you? Have you ever related it to anyone other than Jesus?

6. Is there any way you can change your life or your daily schedule to allow more time for meditation and contemplation and yet still perform your responsibilities to family, your profession, et cetera?

Chapter Two

1. How can you remove the sense of struggle from your life?

2. Is your goal to balance more than 51 percent of your karma?

> *Even though we have been offered the dispensation of ascending with only 51 percent of our karma balanced, it is much more difficult and time consuming to balance the remaining 49 percent from the inner planes after our ascension. I, for one, am trying to balance just as much of my karma as I possibly can while I am still in physical embodiment.*
>
> *We have been told that when we are in the ascended state we still must contact people on earth and yet we have no means of reaching them physically. The metaphor that was used to explain it to me was that we had to lift a glass of water with no hands. Therefore, we can only reach those who are receptive to higher vibrations.*

*So work as hard as you can while you are still in physical
embodiment to balance as much of your karma as possible.
Don't stop at 51 percent! Aim for 100 percent! That is what I am
doing.*

3.   El Morya says, "Little keys unlock the biggest doors, and
     man must be ready to walk through and not stand hesitat-
     ingly upon the threshold."

     There are many "little keys" hidden in this text and in
     other writings of Serapis. I have included a list of some of my
     favorites. Can you add to them and make your own note-
     book of key teachings, not only on the ascension but also on
     the instruction of the other masters whom you met in this
     book? As you continue to read devotional books, I think you
     will find joy in compiling your own book of keys. Look back
     over it from time to time when the going gets tough. It will
     give you new hope.

     - The ascension in the light is the victorious return to God
       from whence we came.
     - The ascension is the beginning of the kingdom for each one.
     - The ascension is the fulfillment of the will of God
       for every man.
     - The ascension flame is a flame of hope.
     - The ascension is a very present reality.
     - You ascend daily.
     - The path of the ascension is the path of love.
       It is love and the dream of love fulfilled.
     - The ascension flame is more than a flame of white fire.
       It is a thing of joy and beauty forever. It is an endless
       visualization, constantly moving, constantly changing,
       spiraling upward.
     - The ascension is God's desire for every man.
     - The ascension in the light is the goal of all life on earth,
       whether or not all life is aware of it.
     - In order to ascend, you must abandon your past to God,
       knowing that he possesses the power, by his flame and

identity to change all that you have wrought of malintent
and confusion into the beauty of your original design.
Cast aside illusion and be willing, in the name of Almighty
God, to change your world.

* With the ascension, the last enemy, death, is destroyed.

* The ascension must be desired and it must be desired
  ordinately, not as a mechanism of escape from responsibility
  or from worldly duties.

* The ascension currents can hurt no one.

* The flame of the ascension is the key that unlocks the door
  to immortality for every man.

* To ascend is to blend in cosmic unity with the heart
  of the Eternal.

* The process of the ascension is one of utter forgiveness.

* Immortality is of a high price, and it demands the allness
  of men from the smallness of men.

* The way of escape for every man is the path of the ascension.
  This is the gift of God to each one, whether men realize it or
  not.

* Let all understand that the ascension is won just as much
  by good works and devotion to God, by service to our
  fellowman, by service to the light, by decrees offered on
  behalf of mankind, and by the many avenues of the
  Brotherhood as it is won by direct study of the mechanical
  process in the ascension itself.

* The ascension is an inevitable part of the divine system.

* The ascension is the capstone on the Pyramid of Life.

Chapter Three

1. Read *Lords of the Seven Rays*. (See the bibliography, page
   254.) This gives a full biography of the many ascended
   masters and their service.

2. You may want to read *The Count of Saint-Germain*, by
   Isabel Cooper-Oakley (Blauvelt, N.Y.: Rudolf Steiner
   Publications, 1970). It is an interesting biography of Saint
   Germain's life in Europe and the events it recounts occurred

after his ascension when he was allowed to return to earth temporarily for a specific mission.

Chapter Four

1. Have you printed a card, "I can make it if I TRY!" and placed it in a position where you can see it often?

2. Are you becoming accustomed to letting Saint Germain's mantra sing through your being whenever you have a free moment? "I AM a being of violet fire! I AM the purity God desires!"

3. Do you sometimes feel that you are refusing the initiations that come to you? Do you feel that you have your life pretty much under control at present and therefore it would "rock the boat" if you ventured out into uncharted waters?

> *I know many of my friends, good people, who feel more comfortable remaining where they are in their lives than moving on and accepting new challenges when they are presented. This is not a helpful attitude for the initiate who has his eye on the ascension, because the ascended masters today offer numerous opportunities for progress on the path to the ascension if we will only accept their help.*

Chapter Five

1. List the requirements for the ascension.

2. List any words you do not understand in the text and check their definition in the glossary, pages 241–253.

3. Serapis Bey tells us in the *Dossier on the Ascension* that in the Ascension Retreat at Luxor lengthy periods of meditation are given to the students, sometimes lasting several weeks. Serapis assigns them a single idea to be meditated upon for hours and the full complement of its meaning invoked from the heart of God. With this in mind, take some quiet time now and meditate upon the ascension flame. Visualize this

flame as an intense fiery white that glows like crystal as you listen to its melody, the "Triumphal March" from the opera *Aïda*.

4. El Morya said, "The trek upward is worth the inconvenience." Are you willing to arrange your life in such a way as to make the ascension your ultimate purpose in life?

> *Sometimes visual helps are necessary to keep us tethered to our goal. I have a beautiful picture of Mount Kanchenjunga, a high snowy mountain in the Himalayas, in my room in a conspicuous spot. At the bottom I have printed, "The trek upward is worth the inconvenience"* —El Morya.
>
> *Perhaps you might like to obtain a print of your favorite mountain: The Grand Teton, the Alps, Mount Everest, Mount Rainier, or any of Nicholas Roerich's paintings of mountains. Having a visual reminder of your goal helps when the going gets rough.*

Chapter Six

1. Call to Serapis Bey and the Lords of Karma. Tell them you want your ascension whenever it will do the most good for the world, according to the will of God.

2. The apostle Paul recorded how the indwelling Christ was formed in us. He wrote in Galatians, "I travail in birth until Christ be formed in you. I live, yet not I, but Christ liveth in me." (Gal. 4:19; 2:20) In a Summit University lecture, "The Roots of Christian Mysticism," Elizabeth Clare Prophet gave us the following meditation to practice to draw down the light of our Holy Christ Self into our physical temple and become one with this Light. The ascended masters teach that our Lord and Saviour Jesus Christ is one with our Holy Christ Self. When we faithfully practice the following visualization in quiet meditation, we can accelerate on the path to our ascension.

Find a quiet place where you will not be disturbed, read the following meditation and then take time to center in your heart:

> As you visualize the Christ being formed in you, see this as points of Light coming together in concentration, originally dispersed and vapory with no form or shape. As you begin to know who is Christ and what is Christ, his attributes, his works, his words, as he lives daily, there is forming in you your concept of Christ, your image of Christ, the Christ whom you adore and whom you worship, the Christ who is your brother and teacher and friend.
>
> And so each day that Christ is being formed in you, becoming more concentrated as Light until the very presence and outline and truly the form of your Holy Christ Self is duplicated here below.

Along with this meditation you may wish to read *The Imitation of Christ* by Thomas à Kempis to assist you in forming a clear concept of the image of Christ.

Chapter Seven

1. The masters have told us that they can send their radiation through their photograph or statue. Do you have a small photo or statue of Kuan Yin on your meditation table or altar?

2. Meditate on these words spoken by Kuan Yin:

Sunder Unreality

Sunder unreality
O mercy's flame of thee
Revere our pure Reality
And set each soul now free!
The flame begins to change the form
From captive to released
And drops of Life's great mercy flame
Infuse the soul with peace.

The love of God inflames the heart
The soul does mold the form
As Wisdom beams the Spirit-sparks

That make each one reborn.
I AM the servant of the poor
The guardian of the pure
My name is Mercy by the Lord
Whose grace let all adore!

Chapter Eight

1. The Goddess of Purity's decree is an excellent decree to memorize and repeat several times a day—in the shower, while driving to work—whenever you have a free moment.

I AM Pure

By God's desire from on high
Accepted now as I draw nigh
Like falling snow with star-fire glow,
They blessed purity does bestow
Its gift of love to me.

I AM pure, pure, pure
By God's own word.
I am pure, pure, pure,
O fiery sword.
I AM pure, pure, pure
Truth is adored.

Descend and make me whole,
Blessed Eucharist, fill my soul.
I AM thy law, I AM thy light,
O mold me in thy form so bright!

Beloved I AM! Beloved I AM! Beloved I AM*!*

2. Purchase a mother-of-pearl shell to meditate on the opalescent, milky-white mother-of-pearl radiance of the Goddess of Purity and the resurrection flame.

3. Repeat over and over again until you gain a rolling momentum of the mantra: "I claim my victory now" or "I claim my purity now."

4. Make a list of simple personalized mantras to help you gain

control over your emotions.

5. Recite to yourself the words to the song, "You Are a Child of the Light" You can also give it in the first person as "I AM a Child of the Light." When you say it, believe it! It is an excellent way to overcome low self-esteem or low self-worth.

You Are Child of the Light

You are a child of the light
You were created in the Image Divine
You are a child of infinity
You dwell in the veils of time
You are a son of the Most High

Chapter Nine

1. Lord Zadkiel told us that the violet flame is the violet singing flame. You may sing this mantra to the tune of "Santa Lucia." If you sing in the shower, this is a perfect time to visualize the violet flame penetrating your four lower bodies and cleansing you just as the water from the shower cleanses your physical body.

I AM the Violet Flame
In action in me now
I AM the Violet Flame
To Light alone I bow
I AM the Violet Flame
In mighty Cosmic Power
I AM the Light of God
Shining every hour
I AM the Violet Flame
Blazing like a sun
I AM God's Sacred power
Freeing every one

2. Here is a violet flame mantra you can use to call upon the law of forgiveness for all of your sins, past and present. You may add to it a prayer for all whom you have ever wronged

and all who you think have ever wronged you:

> Violet fire*, enfold us! (3x)
> Violet fire, hold us! (3x)
> Violet fire, set us free! (3x)
> I AM, I AM, I AM surrounded by
> a pillar of violet flame*
> I AM, I AM, I AM abounding in
> Pure love for God's great name,
> I AM, I AM, I AM complete
> By they pattern of perfection so fair,
> I AM, I AM, I AM God's radiant flame
> Of love gently falling through the air.
> Fall on us! (3x)
> Blaze through us! (3x)
> Saturate us! (3x)

*Substitue "Mercy's flame" and then "purple flame" for violet fire and violet flame. Mercy's flame is a pink-violet color and the purple flame contains a deeper saturation of the blue. The violet flame runs the whole spectrum from light lavender to deep purple to the pink-violet of the mercy flame.

3. Another short little mantra that you can easily memorize and repeat is this call for forgiveness:

> I AM forgiveness acting here,
> Casting out all doubt and fear
> Setting men forever free
> With wings of cosmic victory.
>
> I AM calling in full power
> For forgiveness every hour;
> To all life in every place
> I flood forth forgiving grace.

4. Form the habit of writing to the Karmic Board on New Year's Eve and the Fourth of July. The Lords of Karma meet at these times to consider the petitions of the lightbearers of earth.

Write your letter and burn it in a safe place. The masters have told us that as the smoke rises, the angels will carry your petition to the Lords of Karma.

You may choose to write to any of the masters. Your letter should be hand-written in ink, not typed, for your handwriting carries your personal vibration.

5. As Kuan Yin requested, make your Christmas list and give it to her, listing all whom you have not forgiven and all who you think have not forgiven you.

Chapter 10

1. Remember in your nightly prayers to send your love to the elemental beings. They need our calls because they absorb much of the earth's karma and are trying their best to hold back cataclysm.

2. Portia, the Goddess of Justice, said that "There is no injustice anywhere in the universe." Do you have a hard time accepting this? If so, it may help you to remember that we are balancing karma that we made thousands of years ago. What seems to be unjust to us today may be returning karma from a long forgotten situation.

    I have to keep reminding myself of Portia's statement. I have had a difficult time maintaining my weight since my thyroidectomy many years ago. When I see a person who eats twice as much as I do and still remains slim, I have to keep telling myself that there is no injustice anywhere in the universe.

Chapter 11

1. Memorize "The Violet Fire and Tube of Light Decree," and repeat it when you have a minute throughout the day. Be especially sure to call for your tube of light when you arise in the morning and when you retire at night. See this great waterfall of light descend from your I AM Presence and

extend to beneath your feet, bathing your entire physical form in a shower of light and protection.

Tube of Light

Beloved I AM Presence bright,
Round me seal your tube of light
From ascended master flame
Called forth now in God's own name.
Let it keep my temple free
From all discord sent to me.

I AM calling forth violet fire
To blaze and transmute all desire,
Keeping on in freedom's name
Till I AM one with the violet flame.

2. Keep a journal of the times when you truly felt the protection of your tube of light or the intervention of Archangel Michael and his blue-flame angels.

Chapter 12

1. Purchase a violet flame tape so that you can hear the rhythm of the decrees. (See bibliography.) Practice giving the science of the spoken Word with the tape and become an expert at invoking the violet flame to transmute personal and planetary karma.

2. Purchase *The Science of the Spoken Word*. It has more instruction in it than I could give in the text of one chapter. There are also beautiful full color pictures of thoughtforms for your meditations and visualizations. This book is a must for all serious seekers on the Path.

Chapter 13

1. Meditate on your aura and see it filled with light, deflecting all negative projections that may come your way.

2. Keep a picture of Archangel Michael in your car so he can focus his Presence there. Give the Traveling Protection decree often. Give this decree aloud when you are driving your car and silently on public forms of transportation, and visualize Archangel Michael and his legions surrounding you and all mankind with sheets of blue-lightning protection.

Traveling Protection

In the name of the beloved mighty victorious Presence of God, I AM in me, my very own beloved Holy Christ Self, Holy Christ Selves of all mankind, beloved Archangel Michael, beloved Lanello, the entire Spirit of the Great White Brotherhood and the World Mother, I decree for my protection and for those of my family:

> Lord Michael before, Lord Michael behind,
> Lord Michael to the right, Lord Michael to the left,
> Lord Michael above, Lord Michael below,
> Lord Michael, Lord Michael wherever I go!
>
> I AM his love protecting here!
> I AM his love protecting here!
> I AM his love protecting here!

3. Meditate on a picture or statue of Saint Francis as you give his prayer:

The Prayer of Saint Francis

> Lord,
> Make me an instrument of Thy peace.
> Where there is hatred let me sow love;
> Where there is injury, pardon;
> Where there is despair, hope;
> Where there is darkness, light; and
> Where there is sadness, joy.
>
> O Divine Master,
> Grant that I may not so much
> Seek to be consoled as to console
> To be understood as to understand;

To be loved as to love.
For it is in giving that we receive,
It is in pardoning that we are pardoned, and
It is in dying that we are born to eternal Life.

4. Seriously consider how you may change your vibration whenever it is not in consonance with the ascension flame. Invoke Kuthumi's decree "I AM Light" and visualize the white light intensifying within your aura and radiating out to bless all mankind.

I AM Light
by Kuthumi

I AM light, glowing light,
Radiating light, intensified light.
God consumes my darkness,
Transmuting it into light.

This day I AM a focus of the central sun
Flowing through me is a crystal river,
A living fountain of light
That can never be qualified
By human thought and feeling.
I AM an outpost of the Divine.
Such darkness as has used me is swallowed up
By the mighty river of light which I AM.

I AM, I AM , I AM light;
I live, I live, I live in light.
I AM light's fullest dimension;
I AM light's purest intention.
I AM light, light, light
Flooding the world everywhere I move,
Blessing, strengthening, and conveying
The purpose of the kingdom of heaven.

Chapter 14

1. You will find photographs of the Ascended Master Lanello (when he was Mark L. Prophet) and Elizabeth Clare Prophet in *The Science of the Spoken Word.*

2. Keep your Christhood Diary as Lanello suggested.

3. Complete Serapis' assignment: "Myself, What is Real; Myself, What is Unreal." This is more important to your future attainment than you may realize. Periodically check your list to assess your progress. See how many of the qualities you have listed as unreal can be moved to the column marked Real. The violet flame is your cosmic eraser. Use it often to effect transmutation in your life.

Chapter 15

1. Make a habit of calling for the Electronic Presence of a master to be superimposed over you as you sleep at night.

    When I first learned of this dispensation, I immediately took advantage of the great assistance this gave me toward my ascension. I have continued this exercise for years and as I go to sleep, I call for a different master each night and then occasionally to the same one for several nights in a row if I feel that I need more of a particular flame.

2. In the book *Lords of the Seven Rays,* you will find information on the masters, the rays on which they serve and their service to the world.

Chapter 16

1. Reread *The Science of the Spoken Word* and practice some of the decrees that are not included in our text.

2. Do you try to solve everything by yourself? Are you changing this habit and calling to the ascended masters to help you and then letting God in you be the doer?

3. Read a good biography of Gautama Buddha and see yourself following in his footsteps as you strive to attain his Middle Way.

4. Don't forget to write petitions to the Karmic Board and to other masters. Consecrate them and burn them in a safe place.

5. Memorize the Twenty-third Psalm as a way of eliminating fear, anxiety and worry from your life.

Psalm 23

The Lord is my shepherd; I shall not want.

He maketh me to lie down in green pastures; he leadeth me beside the still waters.

He restoreth my soul: he leadeth me in the paths of righteousness for his name's sake.

Yea, though I walk through the valley of the shadow of death, I will fear no evil: for thou art with me; thy rod and thy staff they comfort me.

Thou preparest a table before me in the presence of mine enemies: thou anointest my head with oil; my cup runneth over.

Surely goodness and mercy shall follow me all the days of my life: and I will dwell in the house of the Lord for ever.

6. Study the definition of the cosmic clock as explained in depth in *The Great White Brotherhood in the Cluture, History and Religion of America*. The science of charting the cycle of the soul's initiations on the twelve lines of the clock under the twelve hierarchies of the Great Central Sun is the science of the Divine Mother given to the messengers by Mother Mary and is the New Age Astrology. It charts the cycles of personal and planetary karma that return to us daily as the tests and trials of the path of initiation back home to God.

Serapis Bey is the ascended master who presides over the 6 o'clock line and the sun sign of Cancer on this cosmic clock. We can call to him to help us overcome the negative manifestations of indecision, self-pity and self-justification.

7.   If you still have moments of low self-esteem or self-condemnation, remember Saint Germain's suggestion and affirm "I AM born to win!"

8.   What do you do to restore your harmony when you are upset?

> *Are you gradually gaining control of your emotions? I have found that saying the mantra "Peace be still and know that I AM God," over and over again until I feel myself in control of my emotions is an excellent way to cure myself of those "butterflies" in the belly.*
>
> *However, remember that this exercise must be repeated each time we feel ourselves starting to lose control. It is not a one-time-only prescription. Also, we must be eternally vigilant. We have a split second in which we can take command before we explode in an emotional tirade of anger. There is still time to say, "Peace be still . . . " and stop the outburst if we really want peace in our world.*

Chapter 17

1.   Meditate on the subject of divine love—the love of God, the masters, angels and elementals. For the next few weeks, as you go to sleep at night, ask for the Electronic Presence of the masters who serve on the love ray to overshadow you and teach you what divine love really is. Record your thoughts.

2.   There is an excellent picture of the threefold flame in *The Science of the Spoken Word*. If you have trouble visualizing, meditate on this picture as you give your devotions.

3.   Are you ready to practice the two tests of love? First, practice giving intense love to the God in your fellowman without desiring recognition or thanks. Second, ask God to intensify his love upon you as the chastening that will purify you and prepare you for your ascension.

Chapter 18

1. Repeat over and over "Not my will, not my will, not my will but thine be done" and know that thousands of ascended masters will be chanting that mantra with you.

2. El Morya says that the repetition of "The will of God is good" is the way to bring the subconscious and unconscious mind under control.

Chapter 19

1. Meditate on Archangel Michael's armor before you go to sleep at night. Visualize his armor protecting you as you call for your soul to travel to the Universities of the Spirit.

2. Do you really believe you can ascend in this life? Are you willing to work for it?

3. Visualize Archangel Michael's blue-flame sword and his band of blue-flame angels using their swords to cut you free from all unwanted habits and conditions in your life.

Chapter 20

1. The seven major chakras or centers of light are anchored along the spinal column in the etheric body and govern the flow of energy to our four lower bodies. Here is a list of these chakras, their colors and purpose:
    a. Throat chakra: brilliant sapphire blue. Through the gift of speech we exercise the power and the authority of the spoken Word. This is the power center.
    b. Crown chakra: brilliant yellow. By our intelligence we exercise the illumination of the Mind of Christ. Through this chakra we focus the consciousness of God
    c. Heart chakra: the color ranges from a delicate petal-pink or rose-colored beryl to ruby red. As the most important chakra, it distributes the energy of the Presence to the other six chakras.

d. Base-of-the-spine chakra: Dazzling diamond white light. This chakra contains the pattern of the fiery coil of the ascension and of the flowering of the Mother flame in the four lower bodies of man. The purity of God is focused through this chakra.

e. Third-Eye chakra: emerald green. This chakra focuses the healing light of God. Vibrating the emerald green of the science of truth, it allows us to see the immaculate picture of individuals, of civilizations and of our divine pattern.

f. Solar Plexus: Alexandrite purple and topaz sun gold with flecks of ruby. This chakra is called the "place of the sun" and is the place of feeling where we employ the energy of emotion as God's energy in motion in order to focus the peace of God's consciousness.

g. Seat-of-the-soul chakra: amethyst violet. The soul is anchored to the etheric and physical bodies here. It is the chakra of freedom.

2. The text should be used as a study aid. After a period of meditation, you may want to reread it.

3. A picture or statue of Mother Mary on your altar will help you in your meditations. Mother Mary gave us the following prayer as her new age rosary for the Age of Aquarius. If you give this prayer with devotion nine times daily, it will assist you to raise the Divine Mother's Kundalini energy stored in the base-of-the-spine chakra up the spinal altar to the crown chakra.

The Hail Mary

Hail, Mary full of grace
The Lord is with thee
Blessed art thou among women
And blessed is the fruit
Of thy womb, Jesus
Holy Mary, Mother of God
Pray for us, sons and daughters of God
Now and at the hour of our victory
Over sin, disease and death.

Chapter 21

1. Do you find that you are sometimes impatient? If so, do you know what to do about it?

    Mother Mary said, "Expect the immediate, but be willing to wait in patience in the possession of your souls for the fulfilling of the Divine within you." She also said, "Remember that in this world you must always consider that the manifestation of God is sometimes of necessity tempered by the conditions of time and space. At other times instantaneous precipitation is possible."

2. Have you ever tried to remain joyful for an entire twenty-four hours? Try it! You may like it!

3. Astrea is the Elohim of the Fourth Ray of Purity. Her divine complement is Purity and their etheric retreat is located near the Gulf of Archangel at the southeast arm of the White Sea in Russia. Call to Astrea and Purity's white-fire, blue-fire flame to cleanse and purify your aura.

Chapter 22

1. Be sure to make a will. In it state clearly that you would like your body to be cremated and also tell your family about your desire because often the will is not read until after the funeral.

Chapter 23

1. Did you know you can pass through the initiation of the crucifixion without dying? I didn't until I heard John the Beloved's dictation.

2. List all the endings you want to use in the mantra "I AM the Resurrection and the Life." For example: I AM the Resurrection and the Life of my finances, my health, my marriage, my children, my spiritual life, my goals, et cetera.

Chapter 24

1. What is keeping you from saying, "It is finished?"

2. Listen to the "Triumphal March" from Verdi's opera *Aïda*, trumpeting the victory of your ascension, or to the song, "Celeste Aïda" which is Serapis Bey's keynote.

3. You may wish to do a novena (a nine-day prayer) to the Great Divine Director for God-direction in your life. (See Chapter 18 for instructions.)

NOTES

Preface

1. Ps. 121: 1–2.
2. 1 Cor. 15:50.

Chapter 1

1. Serapis Bey, *Dossier on the Ascension: The Story of the Soul's Acceleration in to Higher Consciousness on the Path of Initiation,* recorded by Mark L. Prophet (Livingston, Mont.: Summit University Press, 1978), p. 89; Mark L. Prophet and Elizabeth Clare Prophet, *Lords of the Seven Rays: Mirror of Consciousness* (Livingston, Mont.: Summit University Press, 1986), p. 175.

Chapter 2

1. Exod. 3:14, 15.
2. *Dossier on the Ascension,* pp. 166–67.
3. Ibid., p. 62.
4. Mark L. Prophet, *Understanding Yourself: Opening the Doors to the Superconscious Mind* (Livingston, Mont.: Summit University Press, 1985), pp. 95–96.
5. Gen. 5:24.
6. 2 Kings 2:11.
7. John 14:1–3.
8. John 14:12.

Chapter 3

1. Rev. 7:9.
2. Prophet, *Lords of the Seven Rays,* pp. 165, 166.
3. Heb. 13:2.

Chapter 4

1. *Dossier on the Ascension,* pp. 132, 43, 164–65, 99.
2. John 14:6.
3. Mark L. Prophet and Elizabeth Clare Prophet, *The Science of*

the Spoken Word (1974; reprint, Livingston, Mont.: Summit University Press, 1991), pp. 3–4.

4. *Dossier on the Ascension,* p. 90.

5. Saint Germain, "Studies in Alchemy," in *Saint Germain on Alchemy* (Livingston, Mont.: Summit University Press, 1993), p. 99.

Chapter 5

1. Mark L. Prophet and Elizabeth Clare Prophet, *Climb the Highest Mountain,* 2d ed. (Livingston, Mont.: Summit University Press, 1986), pp. 285, 286–87; Saint Germain, "A Trilogy on the Threefold Flame of Life," in *Saint Germain on Alchemy,* pp. 304, 305.

2. Mark 4:39.

3. Mark 10:21.

4. Matt. 11:12.

5. Matt. 5:18.

Chapter 6

1. *Saint Germain on Alchemy,* p. 97.

2. *Dossier on the Ascension,* pp. 176–77.

Chapter 7

1. Gen. 4:9.

Chapter 8

1. John 8:11.

2. James 4:7.

3. See *Prayers, Meditations and Dynamic Decrees for the Coming Revolution in Higher Consciousness* (Livingston, Mont.: The Summit Lighthouse, 1984).

4. Hab. 1:13.

5. Matt. 16:23.

6. Phil. 4:13.

Chapter 9

1. Mark 13:20.

2. El Morya, *The Chela and the Path: Keys to Soul Mastery in*

the Aquarian Age, dictated to Elizabeth Clare Prophet (Livingston, Mont.: Summit University Press, 1976), pp. 46, 47–48.
3. Luke 3:16.
4. *The Chela and the Path,* pp. 46–47.
5. Ibid., pp. 48–50.

Chapter 10

1. Introduction to *Dossier on the Ascension.*
2. *Dossier on the Ascension,* pp. 109, 164–65.
3. Rom. 3:8.
4. Prov. 4:7.
5. Prophet, *Understanding Yourself,* p. 92.
6. Mark 13:31.
7. Matt. 5:18.
8. Prophet, *Understanding Yourself,* pp. 45–46.
9. Prophet, *Lords of the Seven Rays,* Book Two, pp. 145, 148, 150–51.

Chapter 11

1. 1 Cor. 11: 24.
2. Eccles. 12:6.
3. Matt. 17:5.

Chapter 12

1. Gen. 1:3.
2. Isa. 45:11.
3. Matt. 6:10.
4. Job 22:28.
5. Prophet, *The Science of the Spoken Word,* pp. 31, 25.
6. Ibid., pp. 44–45.
7. Mal. 3:10.

Chapter 13

1. Prophet, *Understanding Yourself,* pp. 11, 93.
2. Ibid., pp. 93–94.
3. Kuthumi and Djwal Kul, *The Human Aura: How to Activate and Energize Your Aura and Chakras,* dictated to Mark L.

Prophet and Elizabeth Clare Prophet (Livingston, Mont.:
Summit University Press, 1996), pp. 44–45.

Chapter 14

1. Phil 2:12.
2. Prophet, *Lords of the Seven Rays,* Book One, pp. 163–64.

Chapter 15

1. Mark L. Prophet and Elizabeth Clare Prophet, *My Soul Doth Magnify the Lord* (Livingston, Mont.: Summit University Press, 1986), pp. 328–29.
2. Matt. 10:41.

Chapter 16

1. Gen. 1:26.
2. Ps. 82:6.
3. Deut. 30:19.
4. Rom. 7:19.
5. Prophet, *My Soul Doth Magnify the Lord,* pp. 322–23.
6. Rom. 8:31.
7. Phil. 4:13.
8. John 21:22.
9. Exod. 20:12.
10. Luke 23:46.
11. Prophet, *Understanding Yourself,* p. 16.
12. 1 Cor. 15:40.
13. Prophet, *Understanding Yourself,* pp. 61–62.
14. *Dossier on the Ascension,* p. 42.
15. Prophet, *Understanding Yourself,* pp. 55–56.
16. 1 Cor. 15:31.
17. Prophet, *Understanding Yourself,* pp. 89–90, 62.
18. Ibid., pp. 94–95.
19. Ibid., pp. 6, 47–48.
20. John 8:11.
21. John 14:1–4.
22. *Saint Germain on Alchemy,* pp. 218, 219, 222, 224, 225.
23. 1 John 4:18.
24. Mark 10:15.
25. Ezek. 12:2.
26. *Dossier on the Ascension,* p. 79.

27. John 5:30, 14:10.

Chapter 17

1. Prophet, *Lords of the Seven Rays*, Book Two, pp. 137, 138, 139, 140.
2. Introduction to *Dossier on the Ascension*.
3. Hebrews 12:6.
4. *Dossier on the Ascension*, p. 30.

Chapter 18

1. *Dossier on the Ascension*, pp. 146–47.
2. Prophet, *Understanding Yourself*, p. 75.
3. Luke 12:32.
4. El Morya, *The Sacred Adventure*, recorded by Mark L. Prophet (Livingston, Mont.: Summit University Press, 1981), pp. xvii, 20, 37–38.
5. James 2:23
6. John 14:10.
7. 1 Cor. 15:31.
8. *The Sacred Adventure*, pp. 6, 27, 30, 20.
9. Ibid., p. 114.

Chapter 19

1. Heb. 11:1.
2. *Dossier on the Ascension*, p. 96.
3. 1 John 4:18.
4. Prophet, *Understanding Yourself*, p. 107.
5. Mark 9:23.

Chapter 21

1. Prophet, *My Soul Doth Magnify the Lord*, pp. 323–26.
2. Ibid., pp. 323, 321.
3. *Dossier on the Ascension*, pp. 32, 34.

Chapter 23

1. Saint Germain, "My Vision for the Victory of the Age of Aquarius," August 6, 1989. *1989 Pearls of Wisdom*. Vol. 32, no. 32; Rev. 21:5.
2. John 11:25.

Chapter 24

1. Introduction to *Dossier on the Ascension; Lords of the Seven Rays*, Book One, p. 178.
2. See *"Watch With Me" Jesus' Vigil of the Hours*, released by Elizabeth Clare Prophet (Livingston, Mont.: Summit University Press, 1987), 44-page booklet.
3. Matt. 22:1–14.
4. *Dossier on the Ascension*, pp. 155, 158.
5. Luke 15: 11–24.
6. *Dossier on the Ascension*, pp. 122–23, 119–20, 178.

GLOSSARY

Akashic records. The impressions of all that has ever transpired in the physical universe, recorded in an etheric substance and dimension known as *akasha* in Sanskrit, meaning the all-pervasive, or space. These records can be read by those with developed soul faculties.

Alchemical marriage. The soul's permanent bonding to the Holy Christ Self, the Higher Self.

Alchemy. The spiritual science of changing the base elements of human nature into the gold of the Christ. See *Saint Germain on Alchemy: Formulas for Self-Transformation.*

Angels. Divine spirits, heralds, messengers sent by God to deliver his Word to his children; ministering spirits sent forth to comfort, protect, guide, teach, counsel and warn in answer to our call.

Archangel. The highest rank in the order of angels. Each of the seven rays has a presiding archangel who, with his divine complement, an archeia, embodies the God consciousness of the ray and directs the bands of angels serving under their command.

Ascended master. Enlightened spiritual beings who once lived on earth, fulfilled their reason for being and have ascended, or reunited with God. The ascended masters are the true teachers of mankind. They direct the spiritual evolution of all devotees of God and guide them back to their Source.

Ascension. A spiritual acceleration of consciousness that takes place at the natural conclusion of one's final lifetime on earth whereby the soul reunites with God and is free from the round of karma and rebirth.

Aspirant. One who aspires to reunion with God. One who aspires to overcome the conditions of time and space through the ritual of the ascension.

Astral plane. The lowest vibrating frequency of time and space;

the repository of mankind's thoughts and feelings, conscious and unconscious.

Astrea. Elohim of the Fourth Ray of Purity; works to cut souls free from the astral plane and the projections of the dark forces. See also Elohim.

Bodhisattva. A being of *bodhi*, or wisdom, who is destined to become a Buddha but has vowed to forgo nirvana until all sentient beings are liberated.

Carnal mind. The human ego, the human will and the human intellect; self-awareness without the Christ; the animal nature of man.

Causal Body. Interpenetrating spheres of light surrounding each one's I AM Presence at spiritual levels; the colored spheres of the Causal Body contain the records of the virtuous acts we have performed to the glory of God and the blessing of man through our many incarnations on earth. See Chapter 11.

Chakras. Sanskrit, meaning wheel, disc, circle. The centers of light that are anchored in the etheric body and govern the flow of energies to the four lower bodies of man. There are seven major chakras, five minor chakras corresponding to the five secret rays and a total of 144 light centers in the body of man.

Chart of Your Divine Self. See Chapter 11.

Christ consciousness. The consciousness or awareness of the self in and as the Christ; the attainment of a level of consciousness commensurate with that of Jesus, the Christ.

Christ Self, or Holy Christ Self. The Higher Self; our inner teacher, guardian, friend and advocate before God; the Universal Christ individualized for each of us.

Color rays. The light emanations of the Godhead. The seven rays of the white light that emerge through the prism of the Christ consciousness.

Cosmic Clock. The science of charting the cycles of the soul's karma and initiations on the twelve lines of the Clock under the twelve hierarchies of the Great Central Sun. The science of the Divine Mother as given to the Messengers by Mother Mary to be the New Age Astrology.

Crucifixion. The initiation that requires us to surrender the human self and replace it with the Christ Self. One of the final initiations on the path to the ascension. See Chapter 23.

Crystal Cord. The stream of God's light, life and consciousness that nourishes and sustains the soul and her four lower bodies. Also called the silver cord. See Chapter 11.

Cyclopea. Elohim of the Fifth Ray, specifically invoked for the intensity of the All-Seeing Eye of God and for the opening of the third eye.

Decrees. A dynamic form of spoken prayer used by students of the ascended masters to direct God's light into individual and world conditions. The decree may be short or long and is usually marked by a formal preamble and a closing or acceptance.

Dictation. The messages of the Ascended masters, archangels and other advanced spiritual beings delivered through the agency of the Holy Spirit by a messenger of the Great White Brotherhood.

Electronic Belt. This so-called belt contains the records of all the negative thought and feeling patterns experienced by the soul throughout her physical incarnations. It is located in a person's aura around the lower part of the physical form, extending from the waist to beneath the feet, somewhat in the shape of a large kettledrum. See Chapter 5.

Electronic Presence. An ascended master's light body, the duplicate of his God Presence, which can be focused in time and space within the aura of a devotee in answer to his call. See Chapter 15.

Elementals. Beings of earth, air, fire and water; nature spirits who are the servants of God and man in the planes of matter. Salamanders serve the fire element; sylphs, the air element; undines, the water element; gnomes, the earth element.

El Morya. The ascended master who is the founder of The Summit Lighthouse and the Lord of the First Ray. See Chapter 3.

Elohim. A Hebrew word used in the Old Testament as the generic term for the Deity. It is a plural noun, but when used as a name for God it is singular in meaning. In Genesis 1:27 we read: "And God [*Elohim*] said: 'Let *us* make man in *our* image, after *our* likeness.'"

Etheric body. *See* Four Lower Bodies.

Fallen Angels. Angels who followed Lucifer in the great rebellion and therefore "fell" in consciousness to lower levels of vibration. They were "cast out into the earth" by Archangel Michael (Rev. 12:7–12), and required to take on dense physical bodies.

Four Lower Bodies. The four sheaths surrounding the soul; the vehicles the soul uses in her journey on earth: the etheric, or memory, body; the mental body; the desire, or emotional body; the physical body. See Chapter 5.

God and Goddess. Ascended beings who bear this title have internalized the God-consciousness of a certain quality; a title and rank in hierarchy.

Goddess of Purity. An ascended lady master of great attainment who serves on the Fourth Ray of purity and the ascension and works closely with the Goddess of Light and Queen of Light as well as with Serapis Bey and the Seraphim.

God Meru. Hierarch of the Temple of Illumination, an etheric retreat at Mount Meru near Lake Titicaca in the Andes Mountains of South America. He and his twin flame, the Goddess Meru, focus the feminine ray for the earth.

Great Central Sun. The center of cosmos; the point of origin of all spiritual-physical creation. The Sun behind the sun is the spiritual cause behind the physical effect we see as our own physical sun and all other stars and star systems.

Great Divine Director. The ascended master whose attainment of cosmic consciousness qualifies him to ensoul the flame of divine direction on behalf of earth's evolutions and lifewaves beyond.

Great White Brotherhood. A spiritual fraternity of ascended masters, archangels and other advanced spiritual beings. The term *white* refers not to race but to the aura of white light, the halo that surrounds these immortals. The Great White Brotherhood works with earnest seekers of every race, religion and walk of life to assist humanity. The Brotherhood also includes certain unascended disciples of the ascended masters.

Guru. (Hindi and Sanskrit) A personal religious teacher and spiritual guide; one of high attainment; may be unascended or ascended.

Hercules. Elohim of the First Ray. See also Elohim.

Hierarchy. The universal chain of individualized God-free beings fulfilling the attributes and aspects of God's infinite Selfhood.

Higher Mental Body. The Christ self, or Higher Self.

Holy Spirit. The Third Person of the Trinity; the omnipresence of God; the cloven tongues of fire that focus the Father-Mother God, also called the sacred fire. The Maha Chohan is the representative of the Holy Spirit to earth's evolutions.

I AM Presence. The Presence of God, the I AM THAT I AM, individualized for each of us. See also Chart of Your Divine Self.

I AM THAT I AM. The name of God (Exod. 3:13–15).

Karma. Sanskrit, meaning act, work or deed. The consequences of one's thoughts, words and deeds of this life and previous lives; the law of cause and effect, which decrees that whatever we do comes full circle to our doorstep for resolution. The law of karma necessitates the soul's reincarnation so that she can pay the debt for, or "balance," her misuses of God's light, energy and consciousness.

Karmic Board. See Lords of Karma.

Keeper of the Scrolls. The angel in charge of the recording angels assigned to every lifestream. As custodian of the life records of all souls, he works with the ascended masters and the Karmic Board.

Kuan Yin. The Bodhisattva of Mercy, one of the four great bodhisattvas of Buddhism. In more recent representations, depicted in feminine form. Kuan Yin radiates the qualities of mercy, forgiveness and compassion to the evolutions of earth from her etheric temple over Peking, China.

Kundalini. The sleeping spiritual force in every human being that lies coiled at the base of the spine. When awakened, this sacred fire of the Mother rises through the chakras to unite with the Father at the crown, denoting the state of enlightenment.

Kuthumi. The ascended master who serves with Jesus in the office of World Teacher; master psychologist; sponsor of youth; Koot Hoomi Lal Singh, also called the Master K.H. who, together with El Morya, founded the Theosophical Society in 1875 to reacquaint mankind with the ancient wisdom that underlies all the world's religions.

Light. The universal radiance and energy of God. Spiritual light is the consciousness of God, the potential of the Christ.

Lord Lanto. Lord of the Second Ray of wisdom and illumination. He conducts classes for unascended students at the Royal Teton Retreat in Wyoming and works closely with Saint Germain for the freedom of mankind in this age.

Lords of Karma. The ascended beings who make up the Karmic Board in order to dispense justice to this system of worlds. They adjudicate karma, mercy and judgment on behalf of every lifestream. All souls must pass before the Karmic Board before and after each incarnation on earth.

Maitreya. Cosmic Christ and Planetary Buddha; Guru of Jesus Christ; called in the East "the Coming Buddha."

Mark L. Prophet and Elizabeth Clare Prophet. Messengers of the ascended masters; teachers, lecturers, writers; founders of The Summit Lighthouse.

Messenger. One trained by an ascended master to receive and deliver the teachings, messages and prophecies of the Great White Brotherhood for a people and an age.

Michael, Archangel. Prince of the Archangels, known as the Defender of the Faith and Champion of the Woman and Her

Seed who stands as the defender of the Christ consciousness in all children of God.

Path of Initiation. The path of graded initiations whereby the disciple pursues the Christ consciousness and attains reunion with God through the ritual of the ascension.

Portia. The Goddess of Justice and Opportunity and the twin flame of Saint Germain. Together they are the Hierarchs of the two-thousand-year cycle of Aquarius.

Retreat. The spiritual home of an ascended master or heavenly being. Retreats are located chiefly in the heaven-world. Some retreats are open to unascended mankind and souls may journey there in their finer bodies in sleep and between incarnations on earth.

Sacred fire. God, light, life, energy, the Holy Spirit.

Saint Germain. The ascended master who is Hierarch of the Aquarian age and sponsor of the United States of America. See Chapter 3.

Seraphim. The order of angels dedicated to serving the flames of purity and the consciousness of purity before the throne of God; flaming spirits of living fire who make their cyclic rounds through the galaxy once every twenty-four hours. We may call to them to tarry with us and interpenetrate our forms as they sweep around the earth.

Serapis Bey. Hierarch of the Ascension Temple and Lord of the Fourth Ray of Purity and the ascension. See Chapter 3.

Soul. The feminine complement of the masculine Spirit, referred to by the pronouns *she* and *her*. The soul is the living potential of God and God is Spirit. The soul can be lost; Spirit can never die. Her immortality is gained through her permanent bonding to the Holy Christ Self in the alchemical marriage and the ritual of the ascension.

Spirit. The masculine polarity of the Godhead; the plane of perfection; the dwelling place of the ascended masters in the kingdom of God.

The Summit Lighthouse. An outer organization of the Great White Brotherhood founded by Mark L. Prophet in 1958 in Washington, D.C. under the direction of the Ascended Master El Morya for the purpose of publishing and disseminating the teachings of the ascended masters.

Summit University. A modern-day mystery school for Aquarian Age men and women, founded in 1971 under the direction of the Messengers Mark L. Prophet and Elizabeth Clare Prophet. Summit University currently holds two-week retreats each summer in July.

Threefold flame. The divine spark, the flame of God anchored in the secret chamber of the heart; the soul's point of contact with her Supreme Source.

Twin flame. Each individual's masculine or feminine counterpart conceived out of the same white fire body, the fiery ovoid of the I AM Presence.

Violet flame. Seventh-ray aspect of the Holy Spirit. The sacred fire known as the "cosmic eraser" that can transmute the cause, effect, record and memory of sin, or negative karma; also called the flame of transmutation, mercy, forgiveness and freedom. See Chapter 9.

Wedding garment. Body of light beginning in the heart of the God Presence and descending around the crystal cord to envelop the individual in the vital currents of the ascension as he invokes the holy energies of the Father for the return home to God. Also known as the Deathless Solar Body. See Chapter 24.

BIBLIOGRAPHY

Books and tapes from Summit University Press for your study.

Dossier on the Ascension *The Study of the Soul's Acceleration into Higher Consciousness on the Path of Initiation,* by Serapis Bey. Recorded by Mark L. Prophet. Livingston, Mont.: Summit University Press, 1978.

The Human Aura *How to Activate and Energize Your Aura and Chakras,* by Kuthumi and Djwal Kul. Dictated to Mark L. Prophet and Elizabeth Clare Prophet. Livingston, Mont.: Summit University Press, 1996.

Saint Germain on Alchemy *Formulas for Self-Transformation.* Recorded by Mark L. Prophet and Elizabeth Clare Prophet. Livingston, Mont.: Summit University Press, 1993.

The Chela and the Path *Keys to Soul Mastery in the Aquarian Age,* by El Morya. Dictated to Elizabeth Clare Prophet. Livingston, Mont.: Summit University Press, 1976.

The Sacred Adventure, by El Morya. Recorded by Mark L. Prophet. Livingston, Mont.: Summit University Press, 1981.

Lords of the Seven Rays *Mirror of Consciousness,* by Mark L. Prophet and Elizabeth Clare Prophet. Livingston, Mont.: Summit University Press, 1986.

Understanding Yourself *Opening the Door to the Superconscious Mind,* by Mark L. Prophet. Livingston, Mont.: Summit University Press, 1985

The Science of the Spoken Word, by Mark L. Prophet and Elizabeth Clare Prophet. 1974. Reprint. Livingston, Mont.: Summit University Press, 1991.

My Soul Doth Magnify the Lord, by Mark L. Prophet and Elizabeth Clare Prophet. Livingston, Mont.: Summit University Press, 1986.

The Great White Brotherhood in the Culture, History and Religion of America, by Elizabeth Clare Prophet. Livingston, Mont.: Summit University Press, 1987.

The Answer You're Looking For Is Inside of Yourself *A Commonsense Guide to Spiritual Growth,* by Mark L. Prophet. Compiled and edited by Elizabeth Clare Prophet. Living-ston, Mont.: Summit University Press, 1997.

The Creative Power of Sound *Affirmations to Create, Heal and Transform,* by Elizabeth Clare Prophet. Livingston, Mont.: Summit University Press, 1997.

Violet Flame to Heal Body, Mind and Soul, by Elizabeth Clare Prophet. Livingston, Mont.: Summit University Press, 1997.

Save the World with Violet Flame! 1 and 2.
   2 audiotapes, 90-min. each

Summit University Press titles are available directly
from the publisher or from fine bookstores everywhere,
including Barnes and Noble, B. Dalton Bookseller,
Borders and Waldenbooks.

FOR INFORMATION
To place an order, request our free catalog of books
and tapes or for information about seminars and
conferences with Elizabeth Clare Prophet,
call 1-800-245-5445 (406-848-9500 outside the U.S.A.),
fax 1-800-221-8307 (406-848-9555 outside the U.S.A.),
or write to
Summit University Press, Dept. 476, PO Box 5000,
Corwin Springs, MT 59030-5000 USA
E-mail us at: tslinfo@tsl.org
Visit our web site at www.tsl.org/supress

ANNICE BOOTH has been a faculty member of Summit University for over twenty years. She has taught classes on practical spirituality, including secrets of prosperity, spiritual alchemy, the ascension, your divine plan and the spiritual dimensions of love and relationships. Mrs. Booth has traveled throughout the world giving workshops on these subjects. She has also authored a forty-eight-part series of booklets on a variety of spiritual topics.